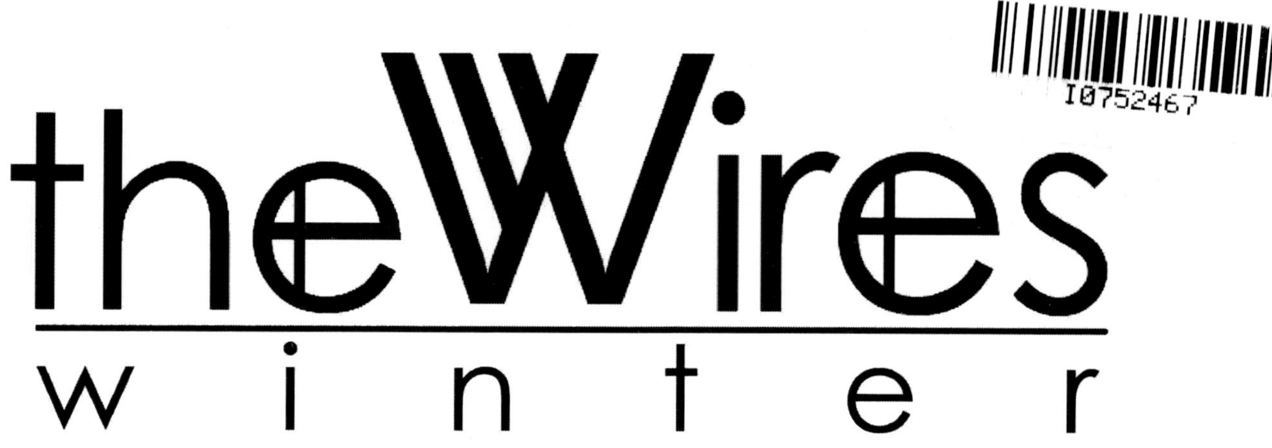

Folk Carols for Violin and Cello

Laurel Parks and Sascha Groschang

VIOLIN PART

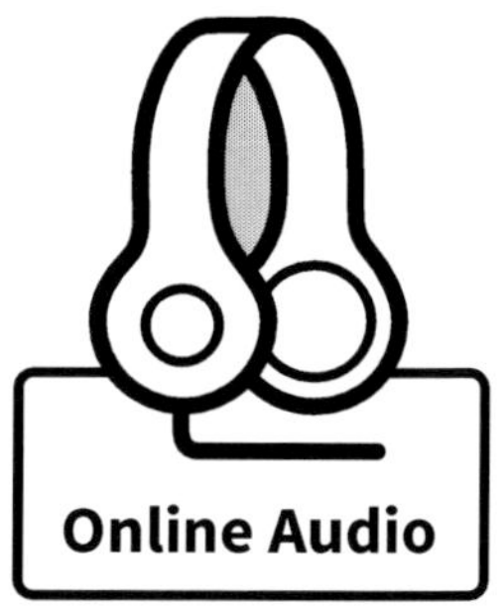

To access the online audio recording by The Wires Duo go to:
WWW.MELBAY.COM/31037MEB

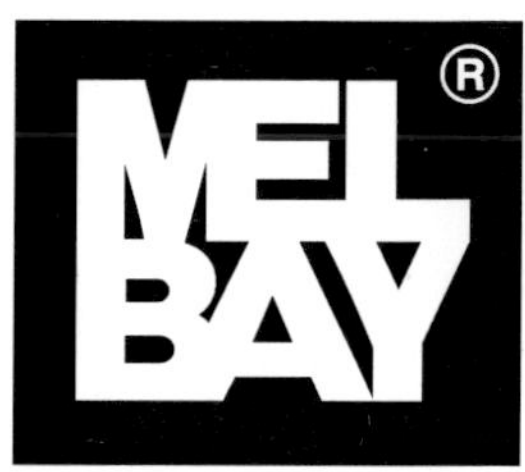

WWW.MELBAY.COM

Contents

Title	Page	Audio

Performance Notes

We've notated many of the ornaments heard on our studio recording "Winter." However, all of these pieces are inspired by folk idioms. Feel free to take away or add your own ornaments, slides and double stops. This music is less rigid than traditional classical music so there is plenty of room for micro-improvisations. In other words, make these pieces your own!

A few specific techniques are used in the cello parts. Several of the tunes use the chopping technique. This technique is indicated by an 'X' notehead. *Greensleeves* and *We Wish You a Merry Christmas* use a strumming pizzicato technique and *We Wish You a Merry Christmas* uses a fingerboard slap, as indicated with a slash notehead.

The chop utilizes a straight thumb and is a combination of dropping the bow heavily on the string and allowing the bow to scrape the strings. Your bow hair will be angled slightly towards the floor, and your contact point will be closer to the bridge than usual. The note after the chop will be a quasi-chop. The act of releasing the bow off the string will create a sort of ghost note, a little bit of pitch will be heard, and a small chopping scrape sound will also be audible.

For the strumming technique, you will use your thumb to pizzicato on the lower strings, away from your body. For the top strings, you will use your 3rd finger to pluck toward your body. For the slap pizzicato technique, you'll slap your fingerboard, allowing the strings to hit the wood to create a nice percussive sound. For each of these techniques, the most important thing is that the groove stays steady, so don't worry too much about perfection!

For video instructions on all 3 techniques: Find "TheWiresDuo" channel on Youtube and search for the "Special Cello Techniques" video: https://www.youtube.com/watch?v=oc34FkDRI_U

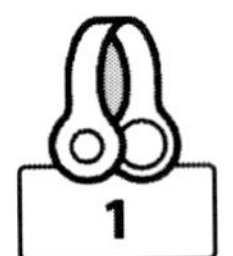

Lo, How a Rose E'er Blooming

Michael Praetorius
Arranged by The Wires: Sascha Groschang and Laurel Parks

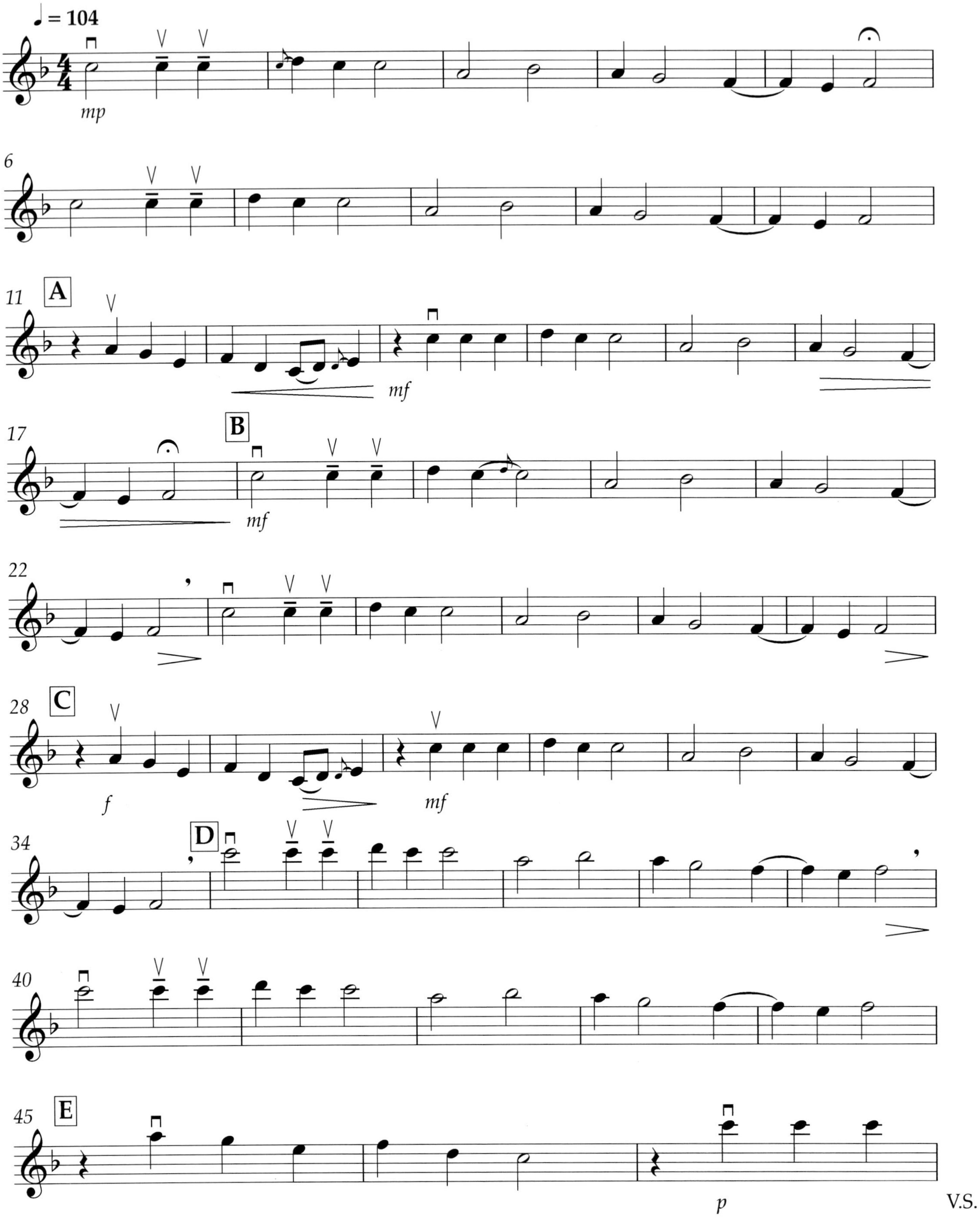

♩ = 104

mp

6

11 A

mf

17 B

mf

22

28 C

f

mf

34 D

40

45 E

p

V.S.

Violin

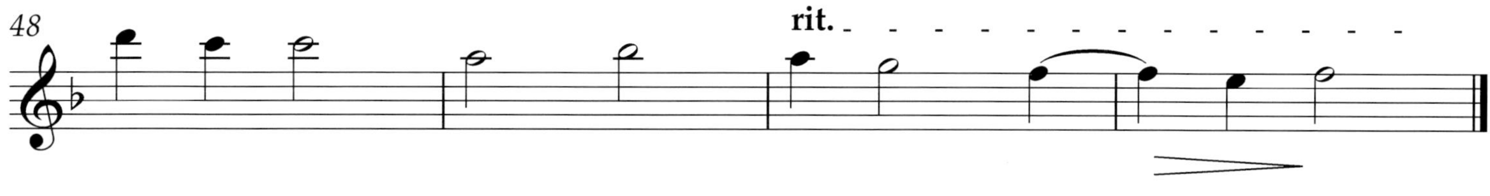

Coventry Carol

Traditional
Arranged by The Wires: Sascha Groschang and Laurel Parks

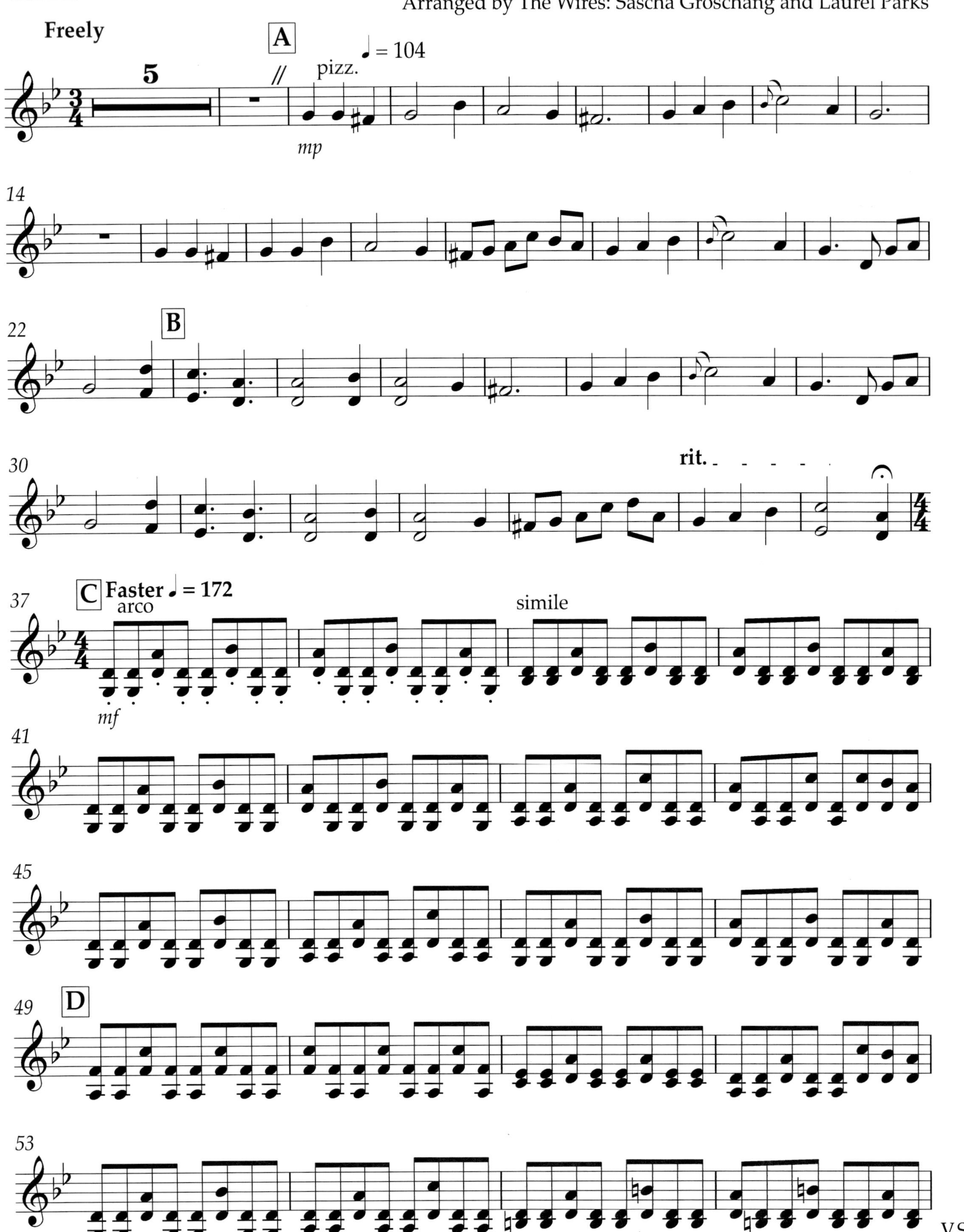

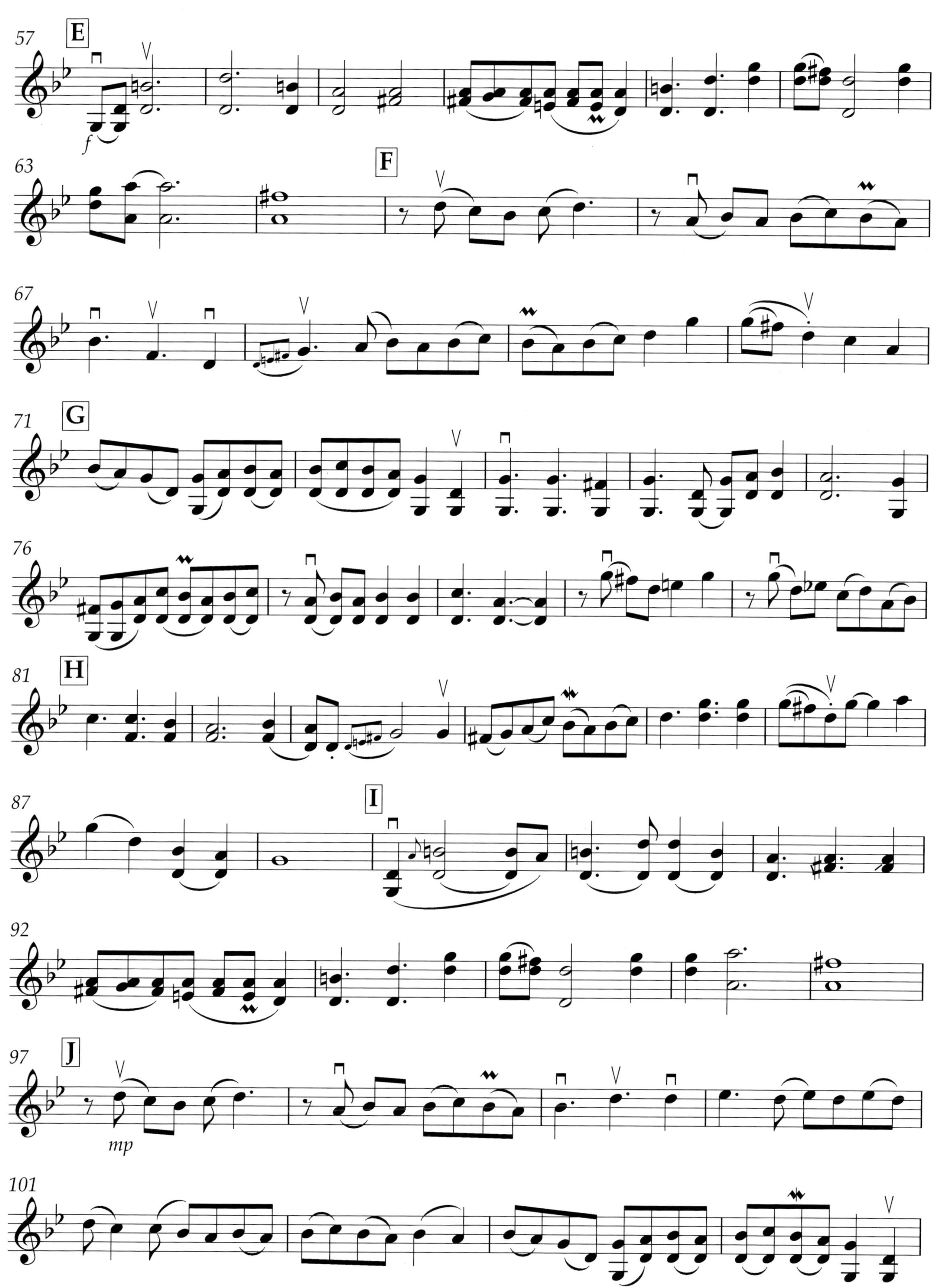
57
E
f
63
F
67
71
G
76
81
H
87
I
92
97
J
mp
101

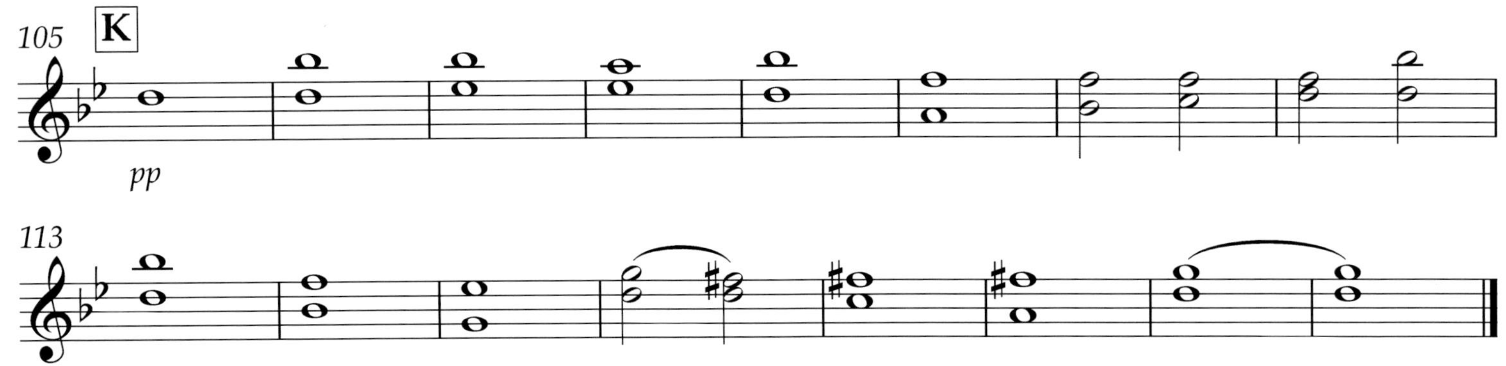
105
K
pp
113

This page has been left blank to avoid an awkward page turn.

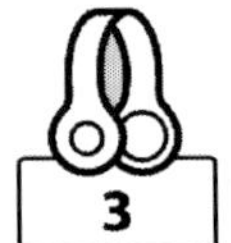

Silent Night

Franz Xaver Gruber
Arranged by The Wires: Sascha Groschang and Laurel Parks

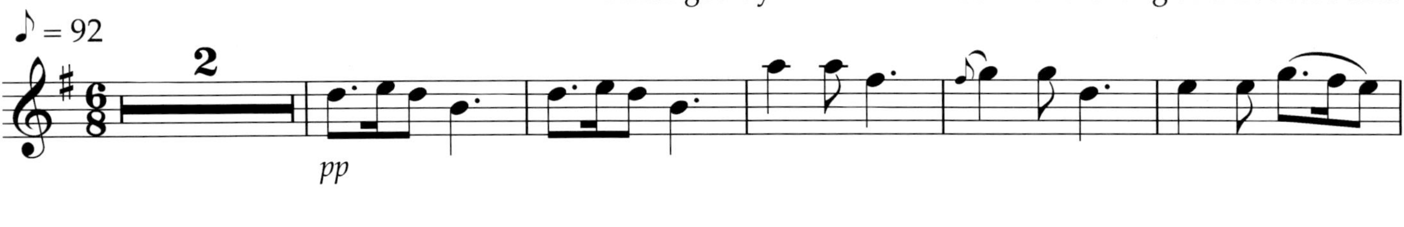

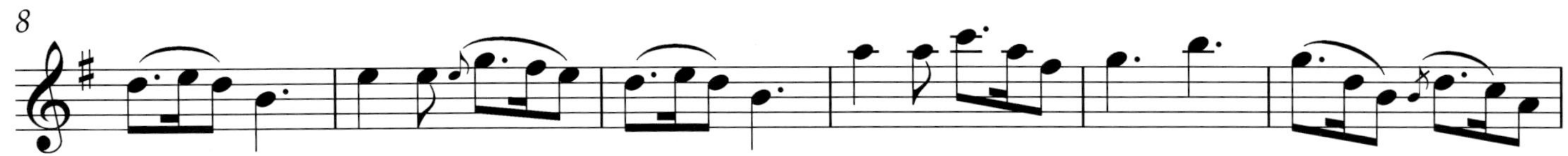

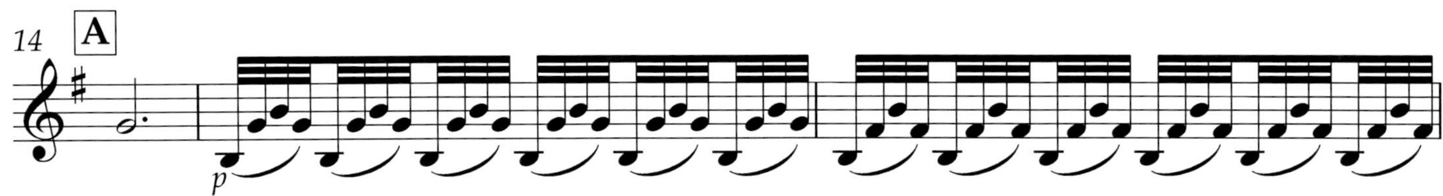

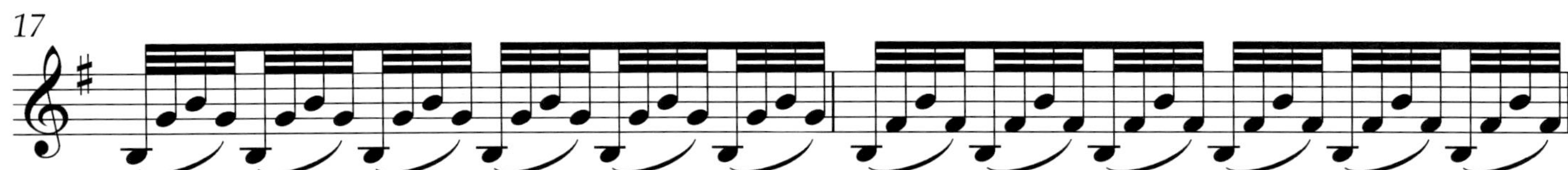

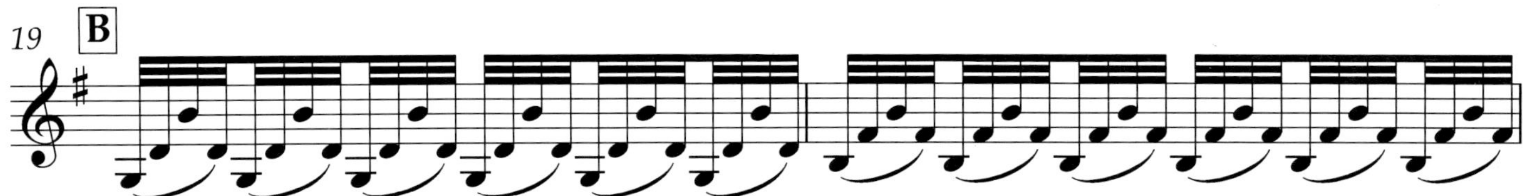

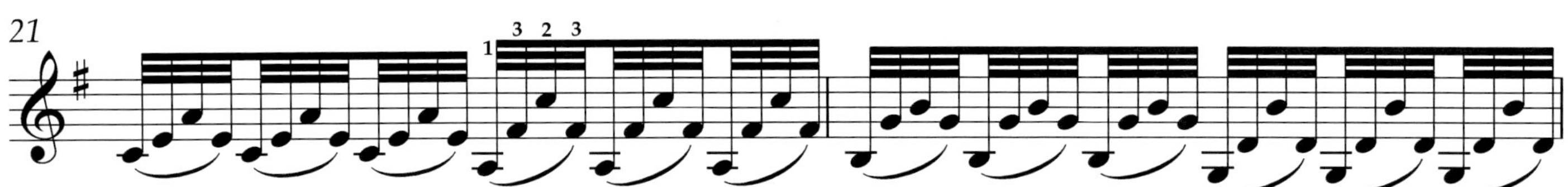

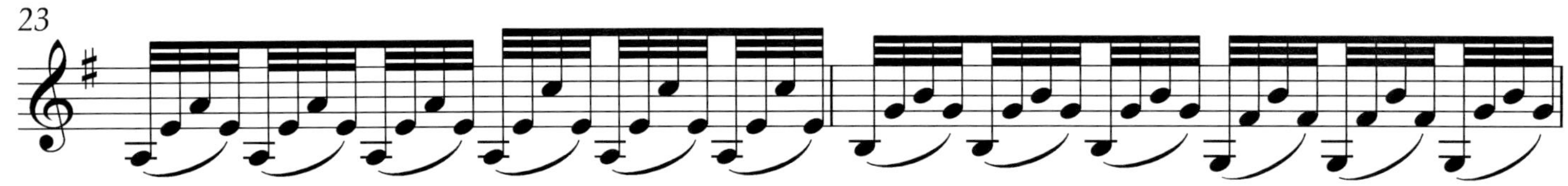

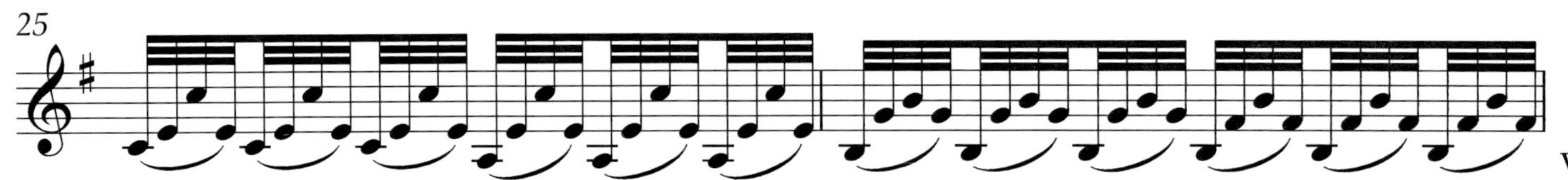

V.S.

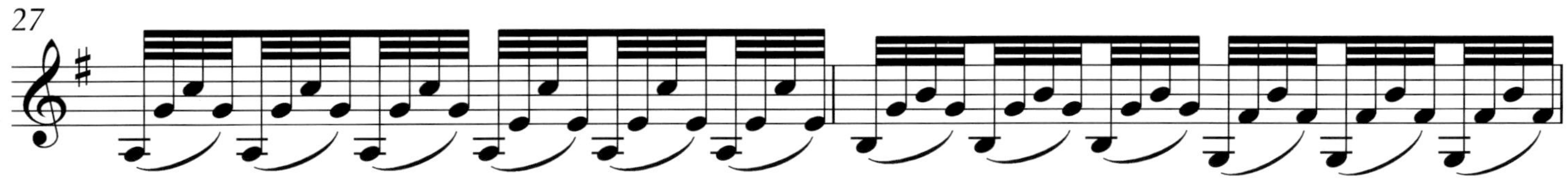
27
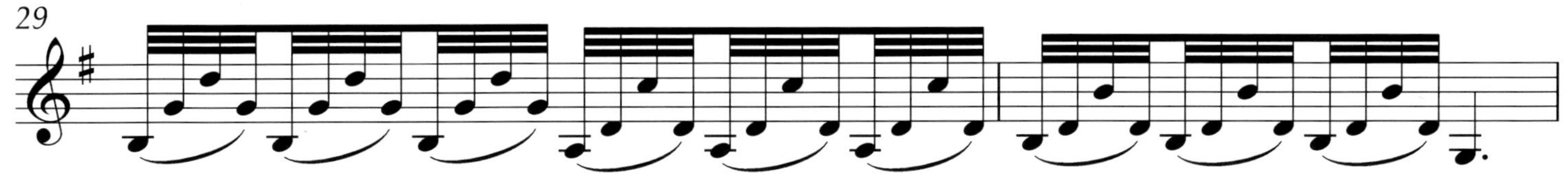
29
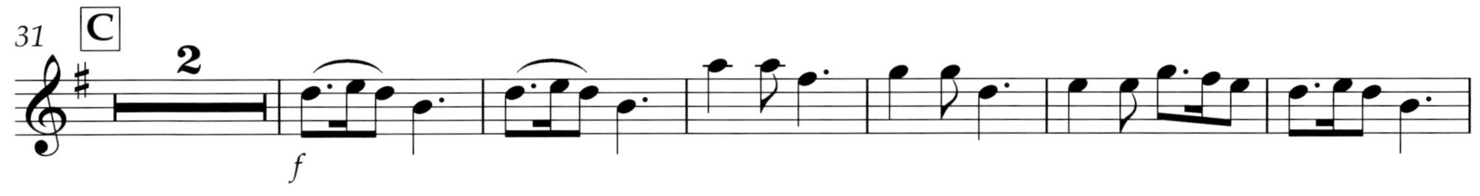
31
C
2
f
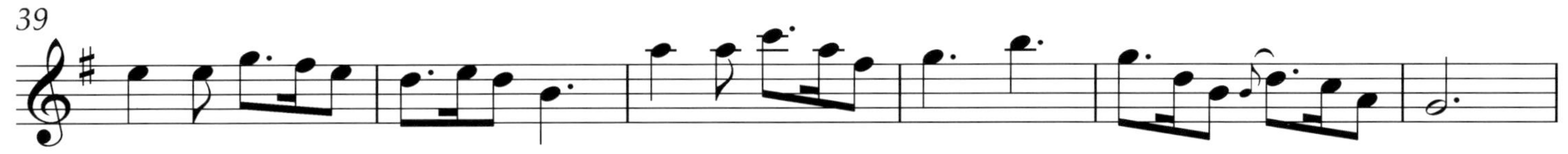
39
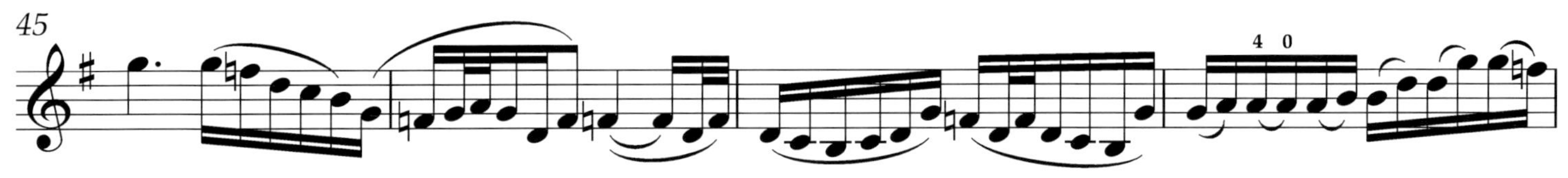
45
4 0
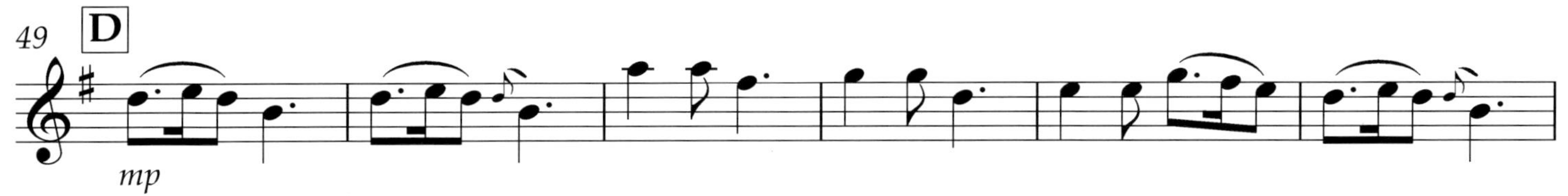
49
D
mp
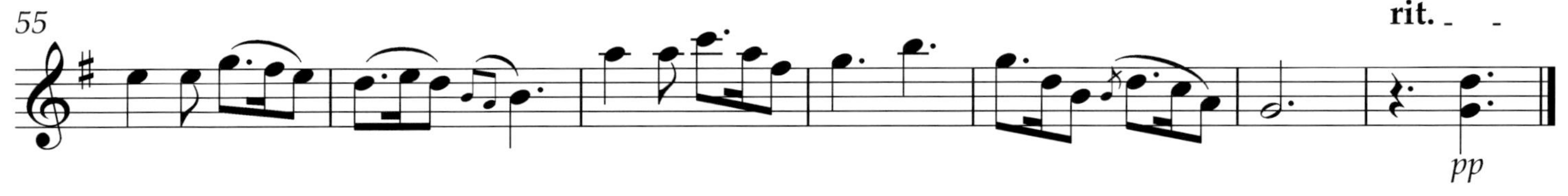
55
rit.
pp

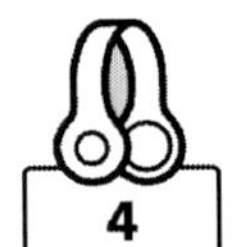

Greensleeves

Traditional
Arranged by The Wires: Sascha Groschang and Laurel Parks

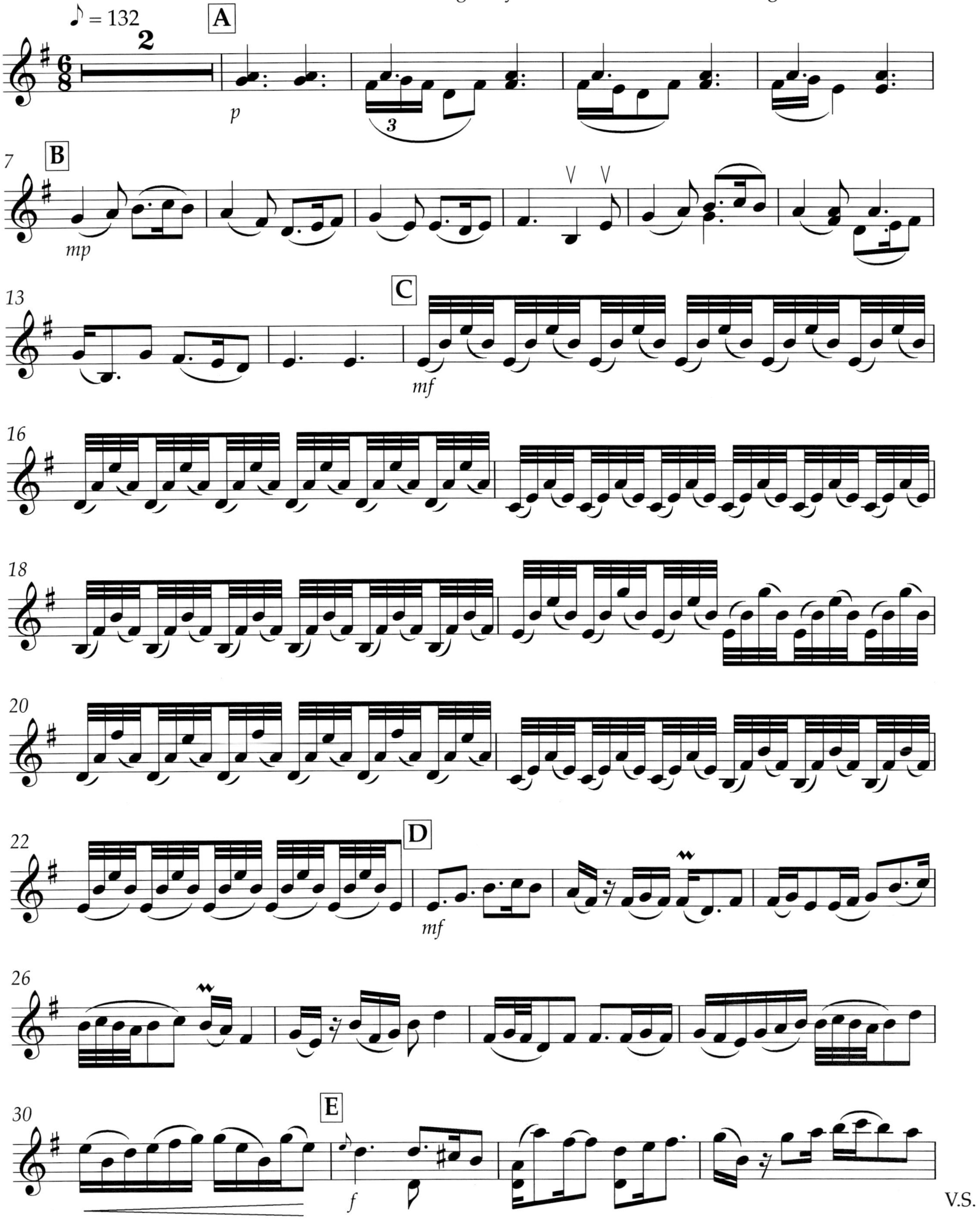

♪ = 132

A

2

p

7 B

mp

13 C

mf

16

18

20

22 D

mf

26

30 E

f

V.S.

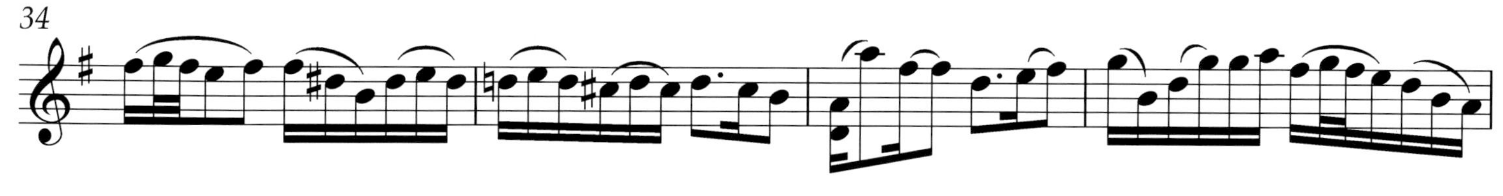
34
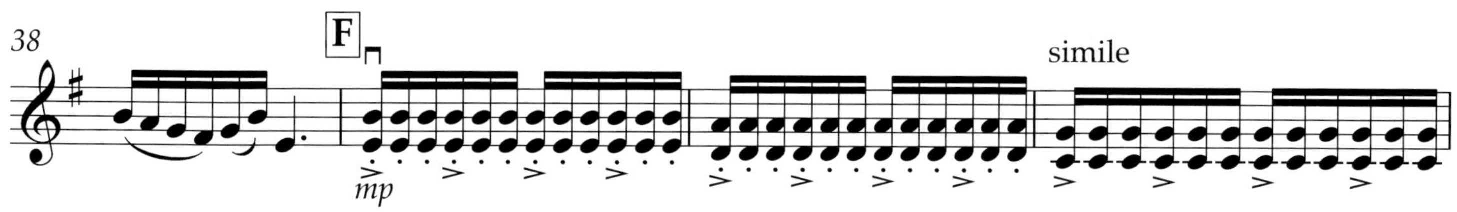
38
F
mp
simile
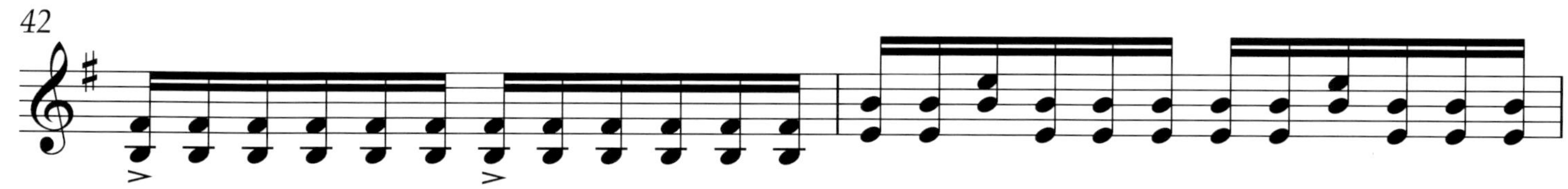
42
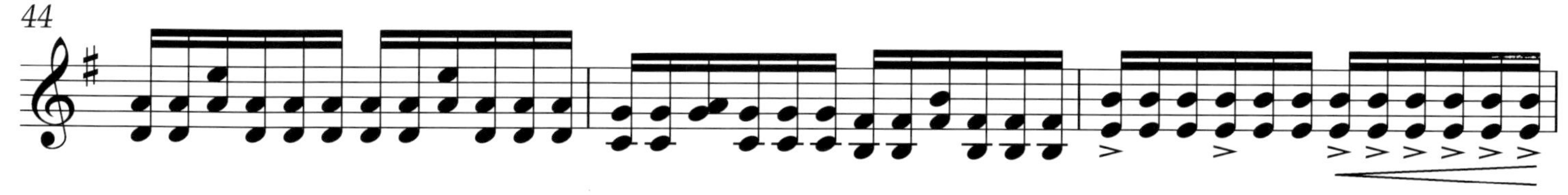
44
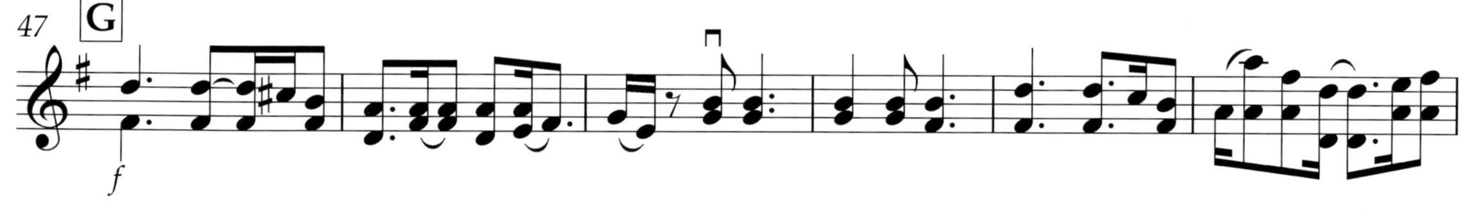
47
G
f
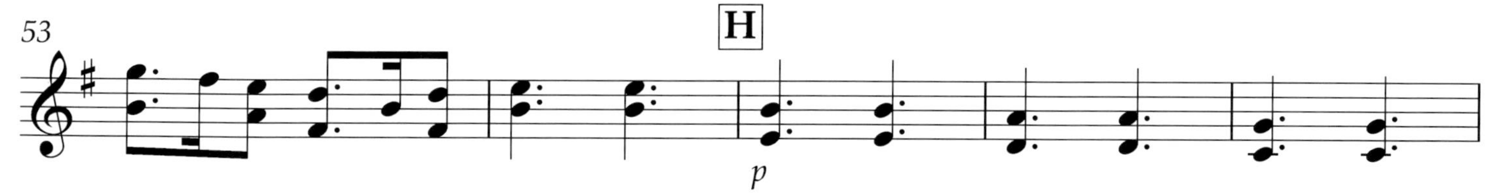
53
H
p
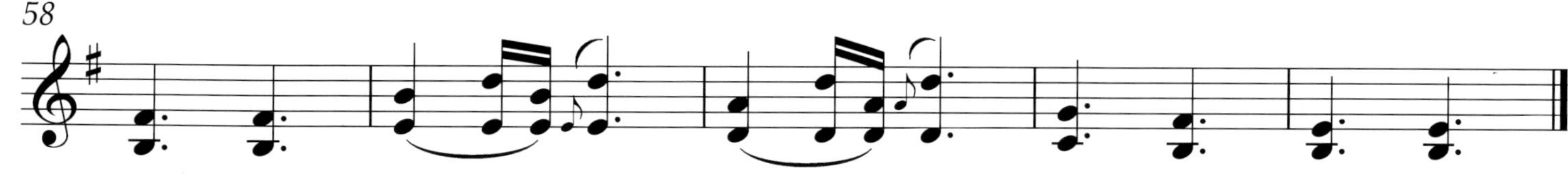
58

The Holly and the Ivy

5

Arranged by The Wires: Sascha Groschang and Laurel Parks

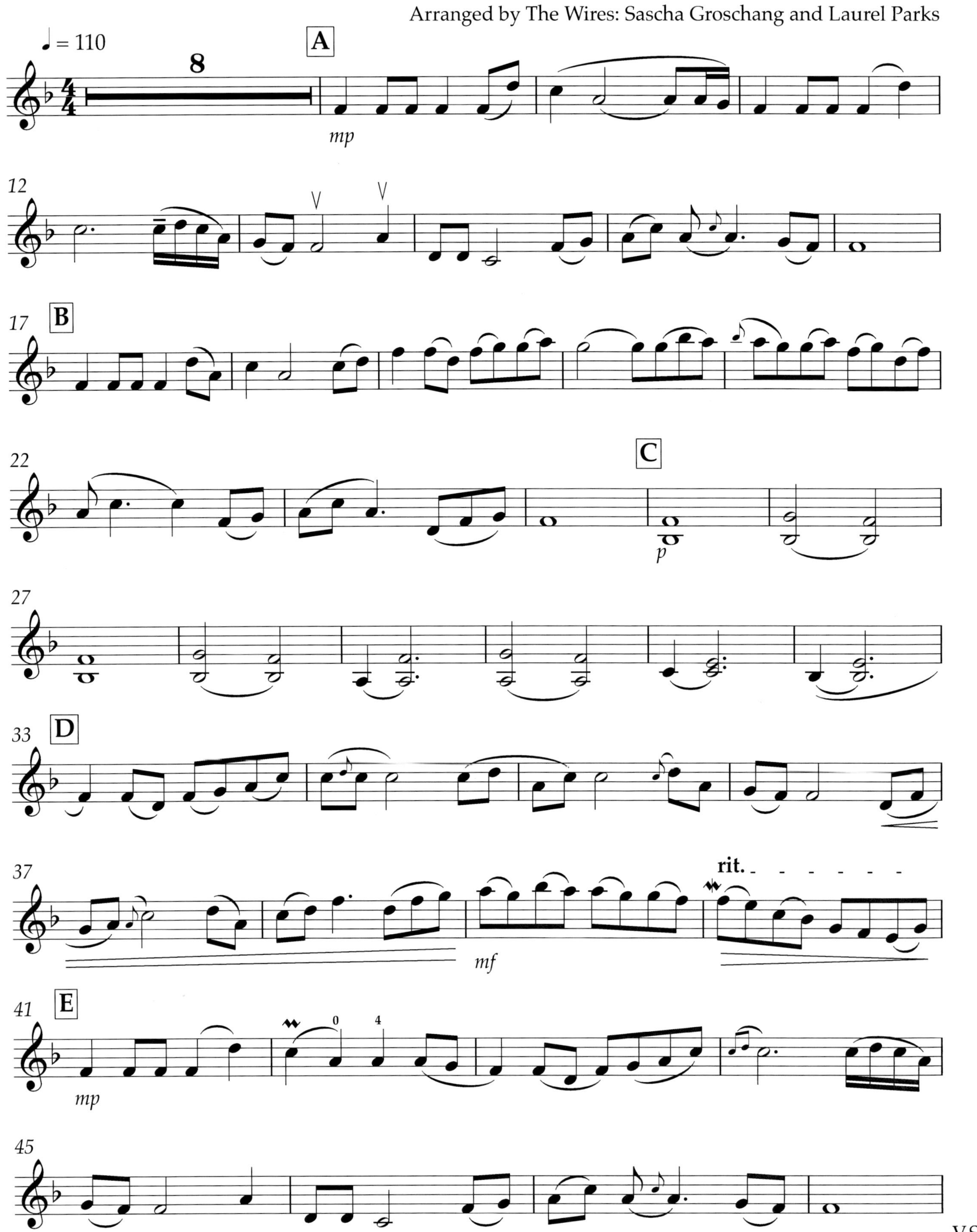

V.S.

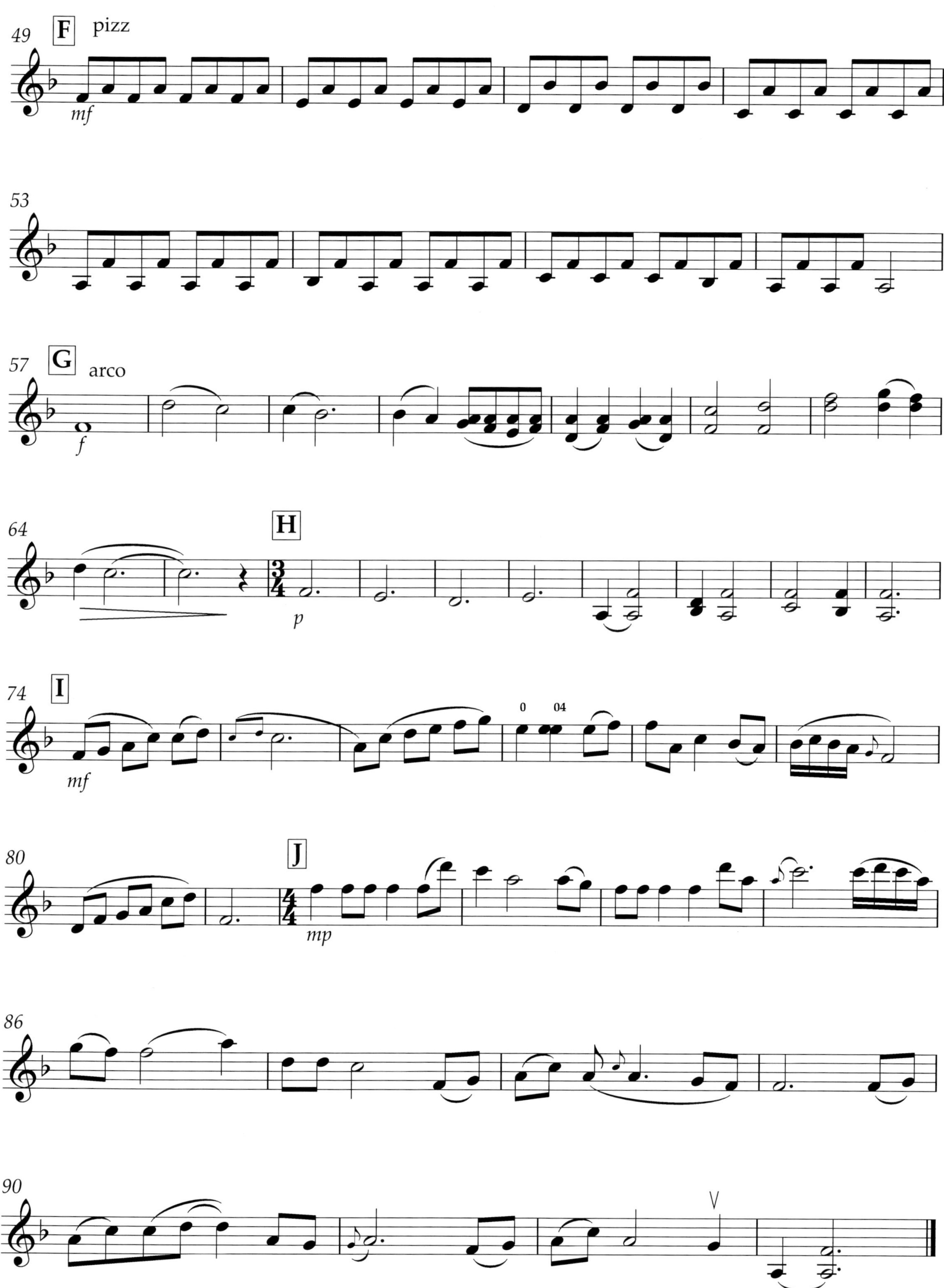
49
F
pizz
mf
53
57
G
arco
f
64
H
p
74
I
mf
0
04
80
J
mp
86
90

Wexford Carol

Traditional English
Arranged by The Wires: Sascha Groschang and Laurel Parks

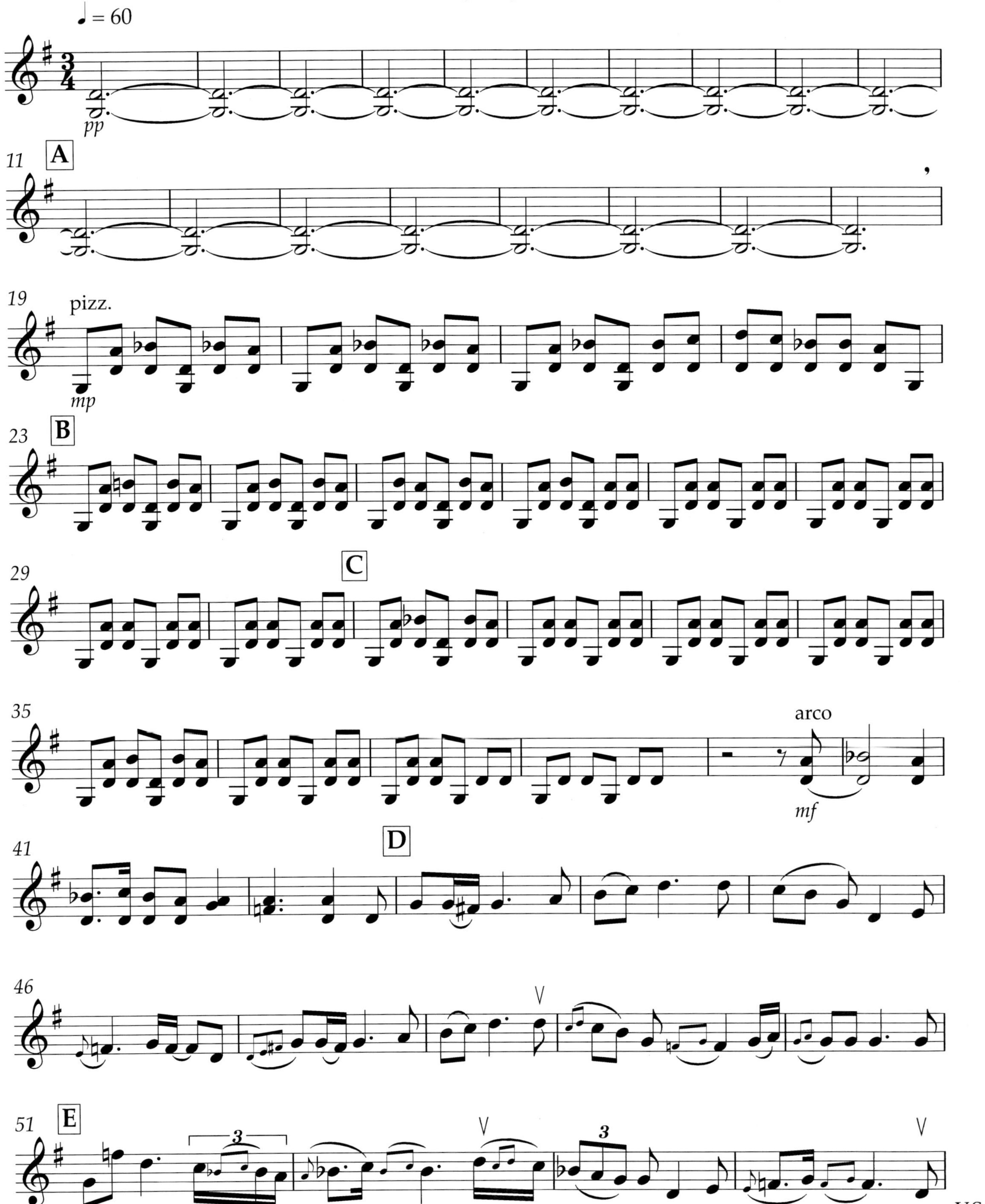

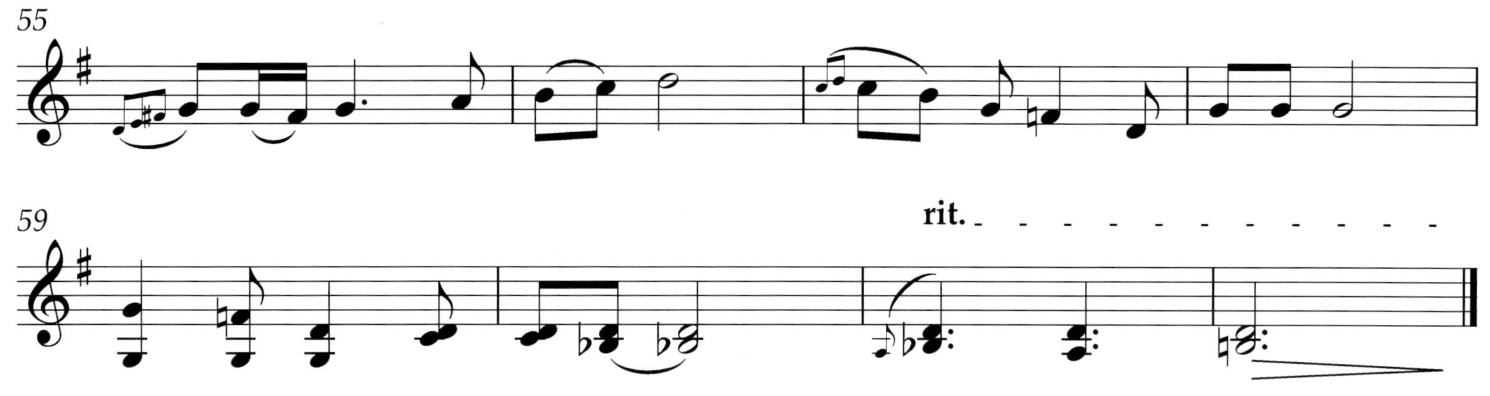
55
59
rit.

Bring a Torch Jeannette, Isabella

Traditional French
Arranged by the Wires: Sascha Groschang and Laurel Parks

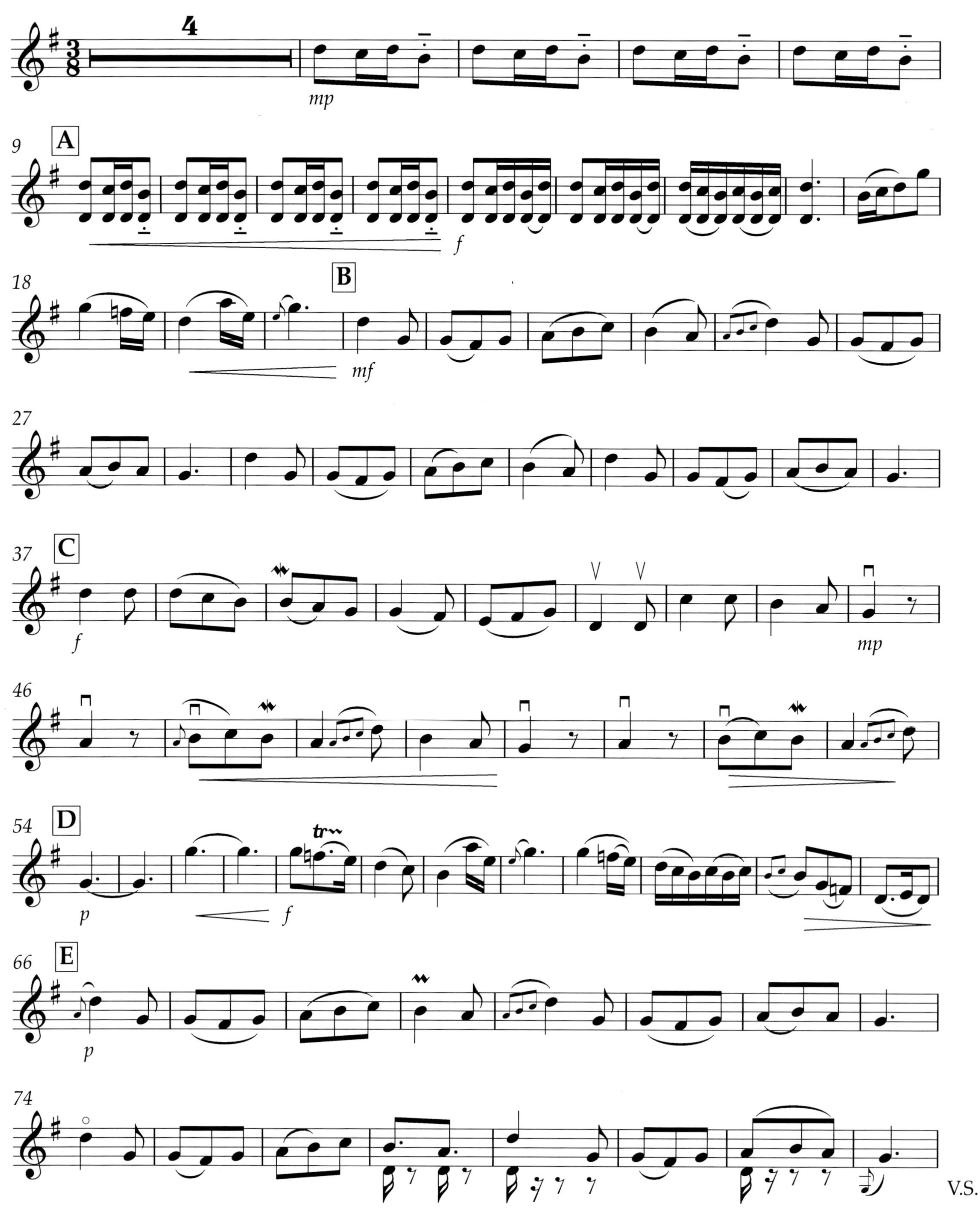

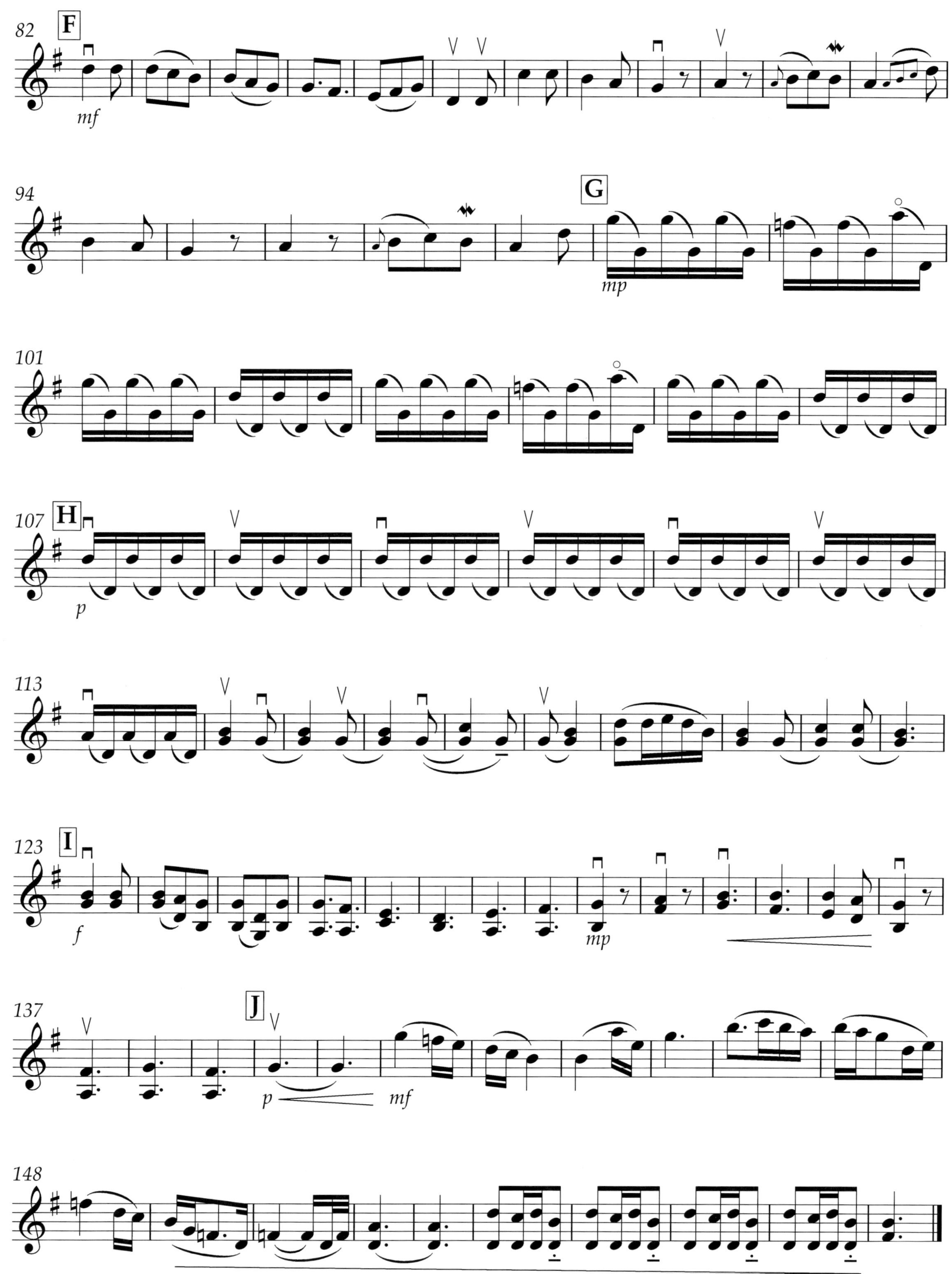
82
F
mf
94
G
mp
101
107
H
p
113
123
I
f
mp
137
J
p
mf
148

In the Bleak Midwinter

Gustav Holst
Arranged by The Wires: Sascha Groschang and Laurel Parks

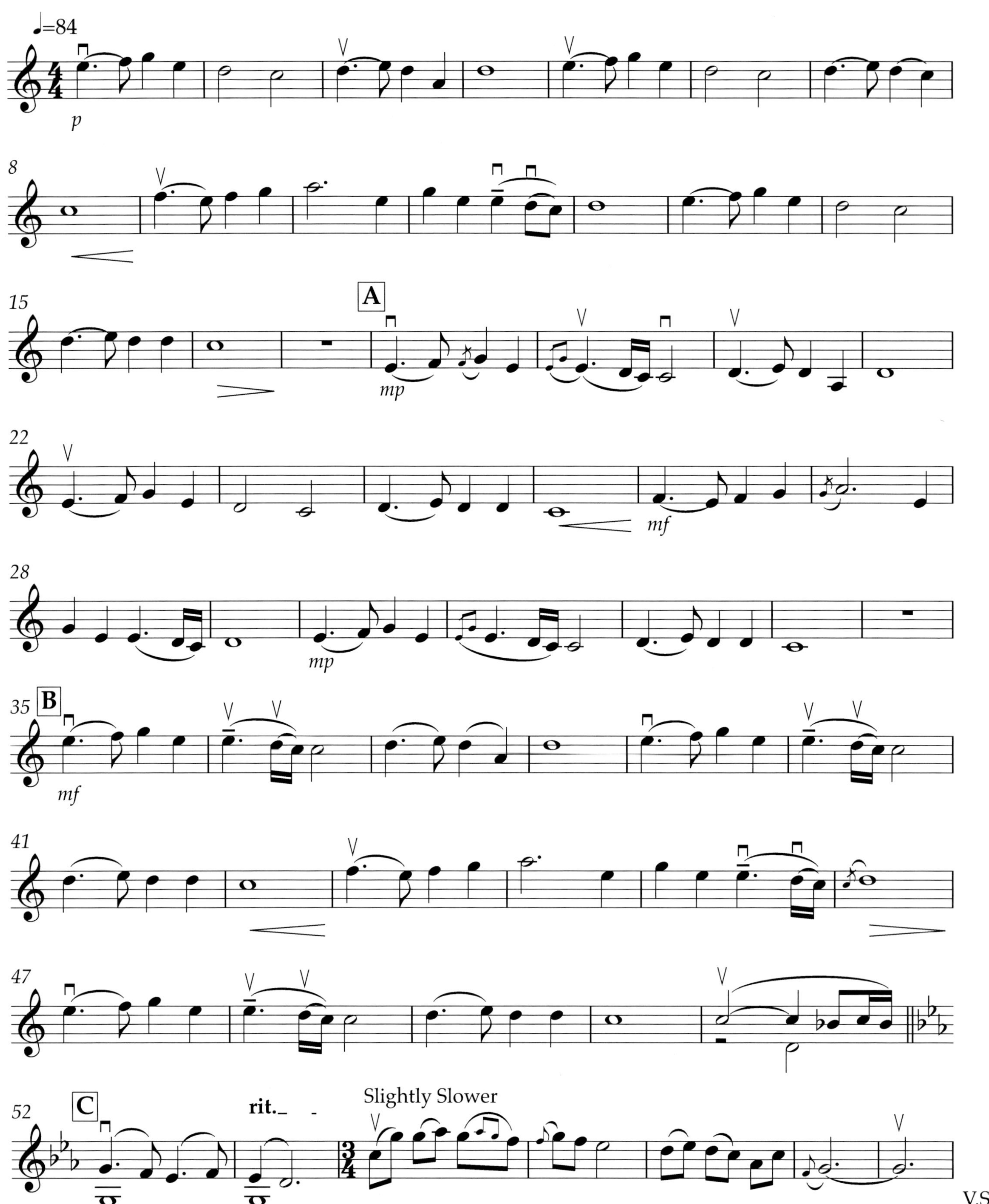

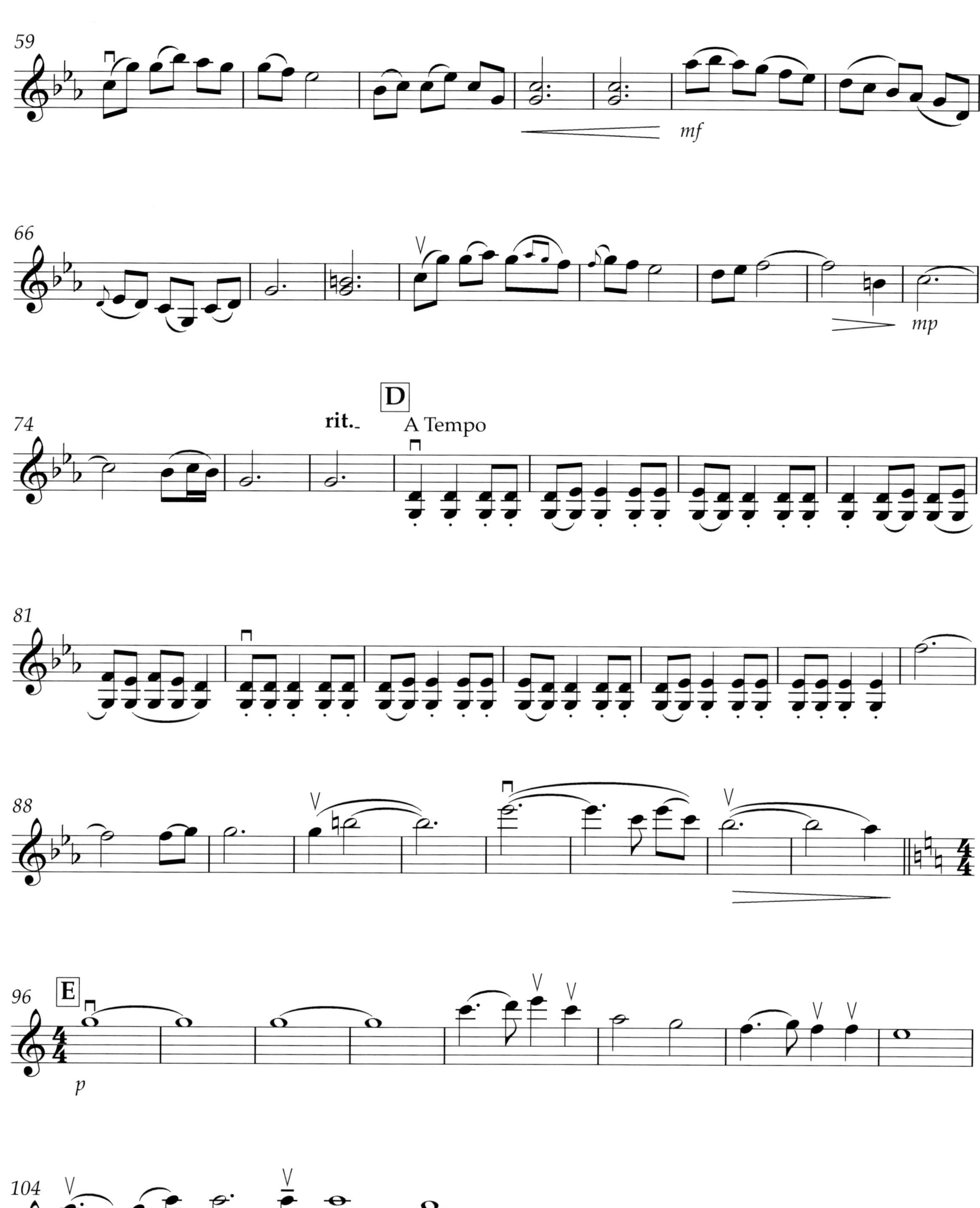
59
mf
66
mp
74
rit.
D
A Tempo
81
88
96
E
p
104
rit......

9

Campbell Street

The Wires: Sascha Groschang and Laurel Parks

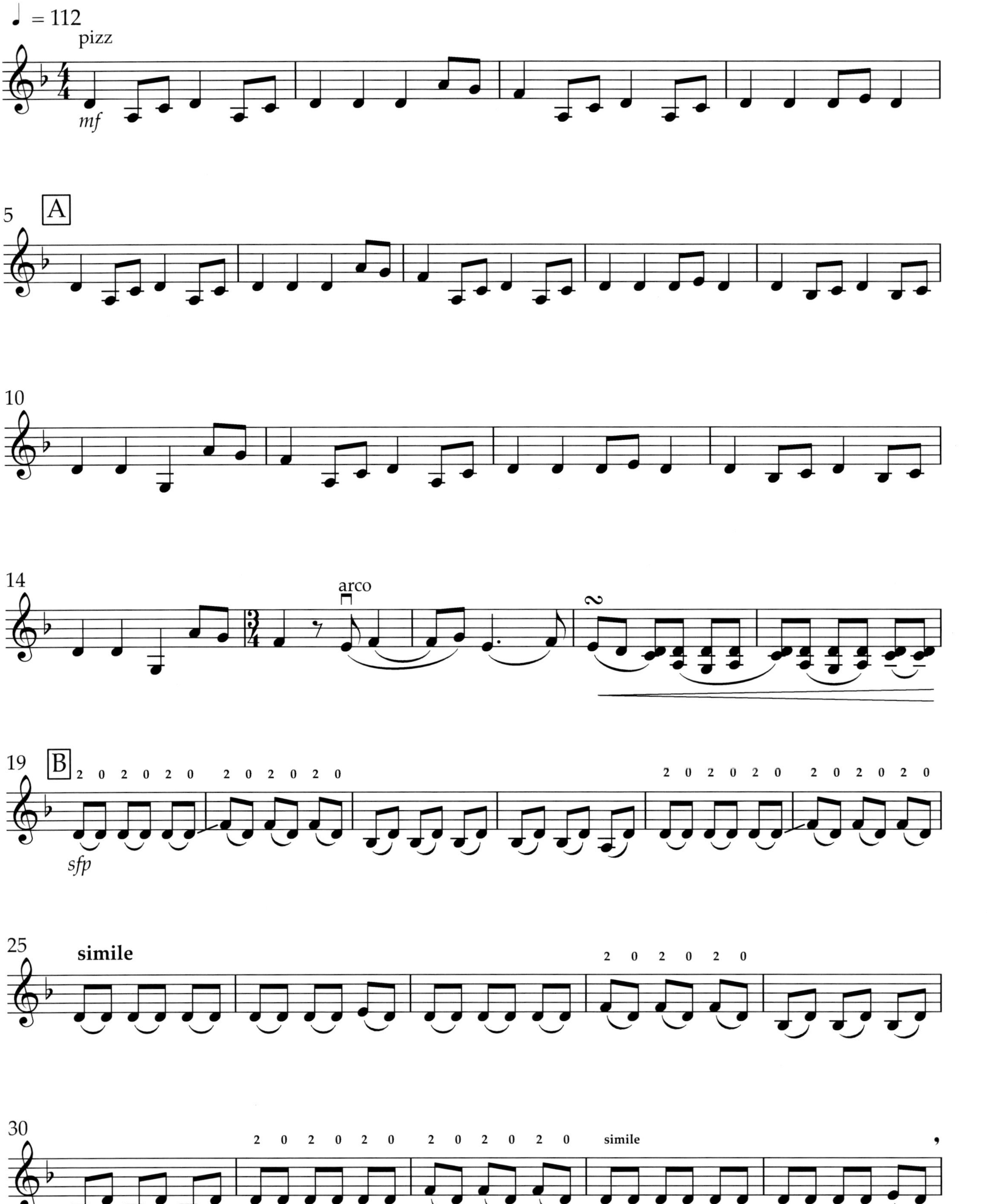

♩ = 112

pizz

mf

5 A

10

14

arco

19 B

2 0 2 0 2 0 2 0 2 0 2 0

sfp

2 0 2 0 2 0 2 0 2 0 2 0

25

simile

2 0 2 0 2 0

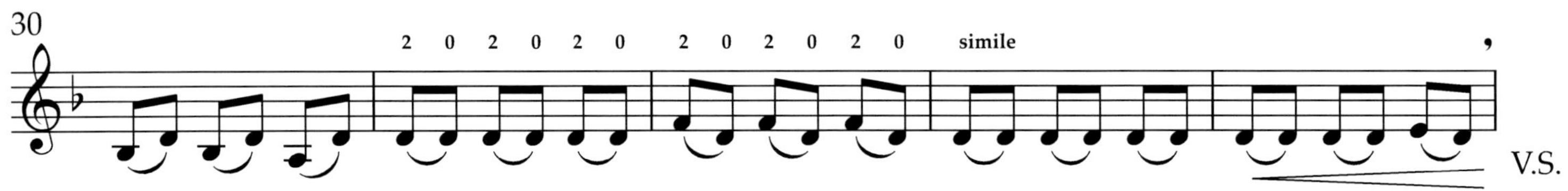

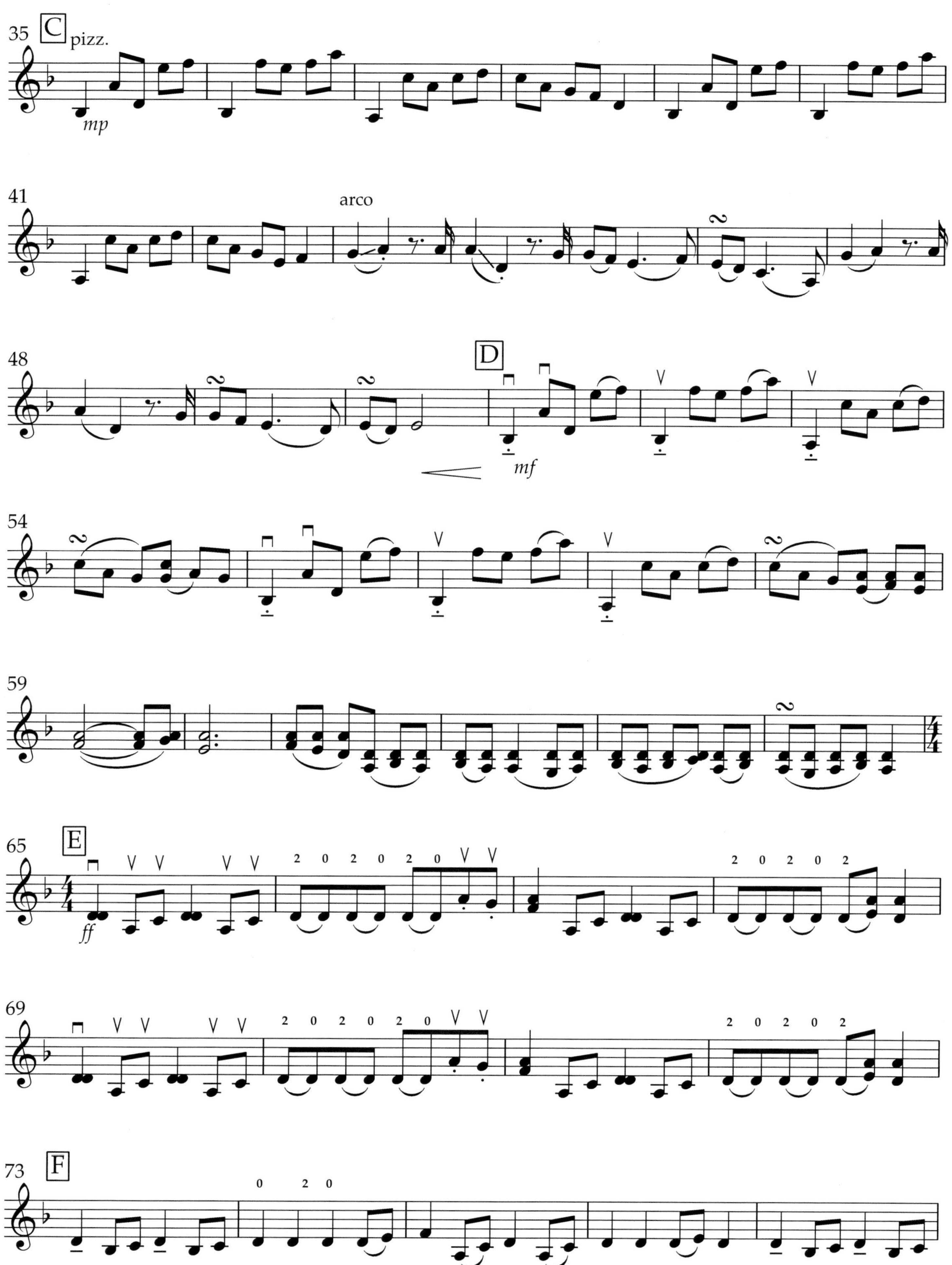

35
C
pizz.
mp
41
arco
48
D
mf
54
59
65
E
ff
2 0 2 0 2 0
2 0 2 0 2
69
2 0 2 0 2 0
2 0 2 0 2
73
F
0 2 0

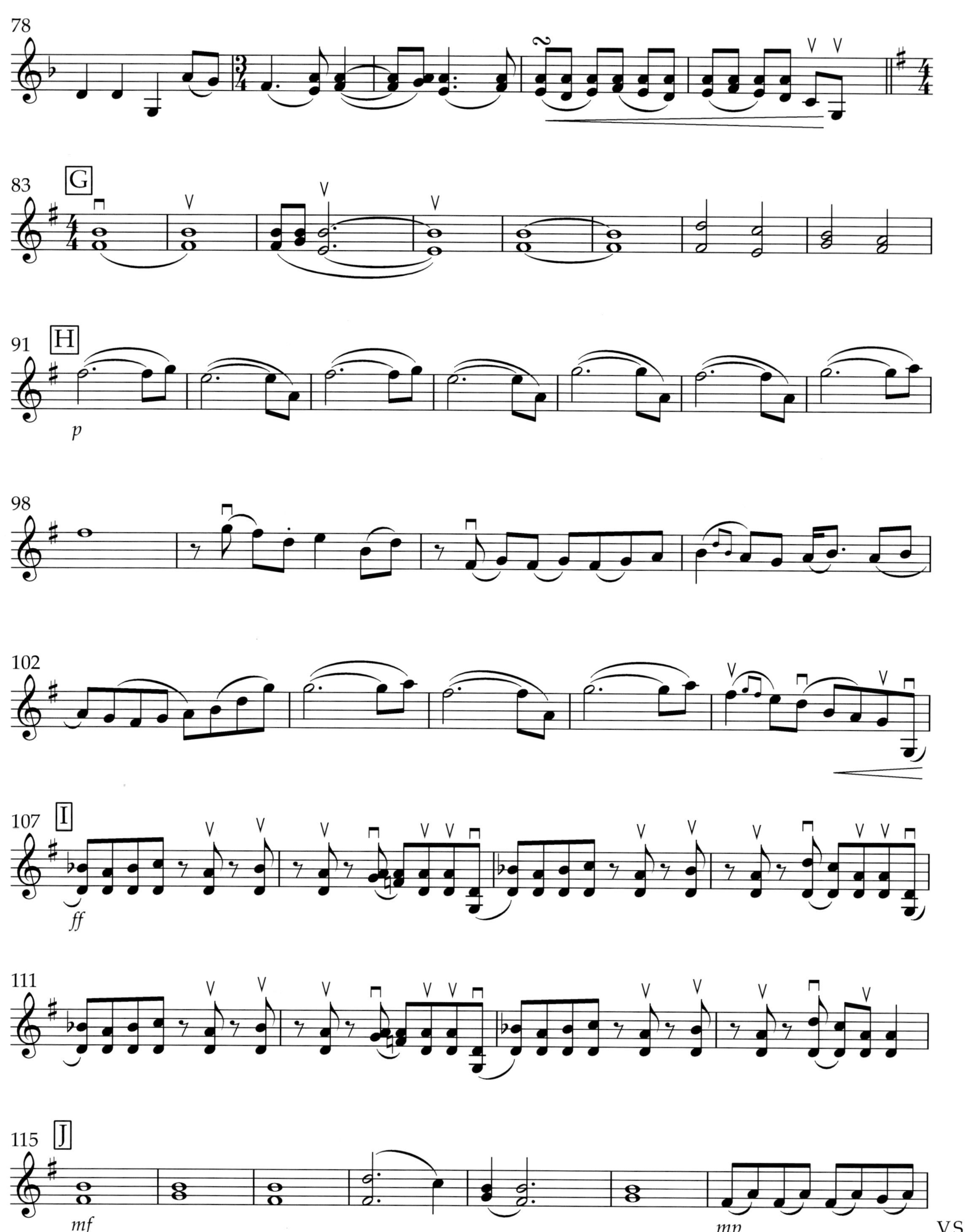
78
83
G
91
H
p
98
102
107
I
ff
111
115
J
mf
mp
V.S.

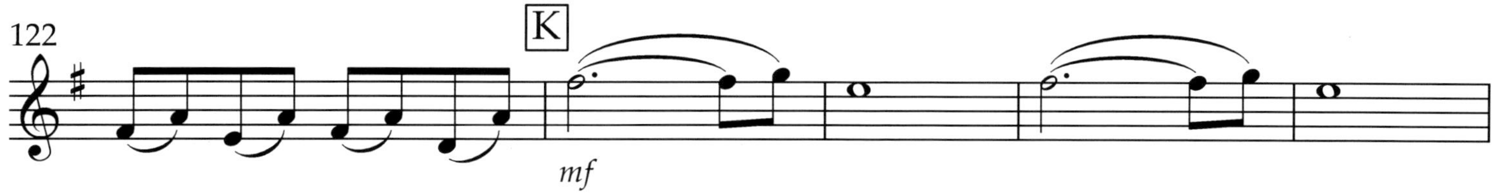
122
K
mf

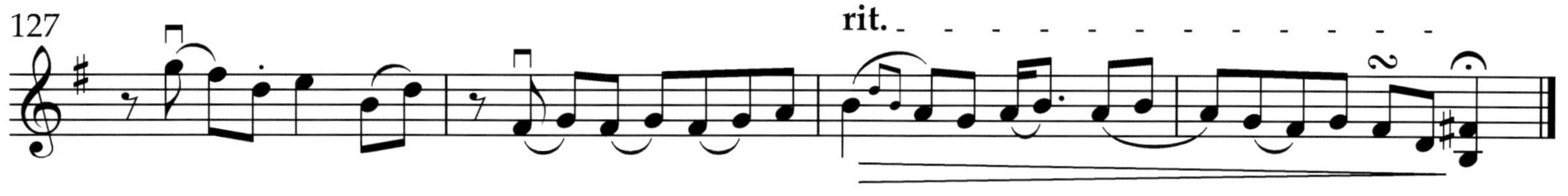
127
rit.

10

Once in Royal David's City

Cecil Francis Alexander and Henry John Gauntlett
Arranged by The Wires: Sascha Groschang and Laurel Parks

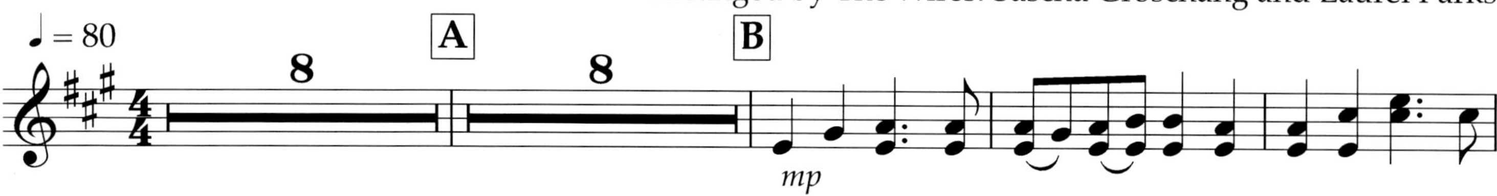

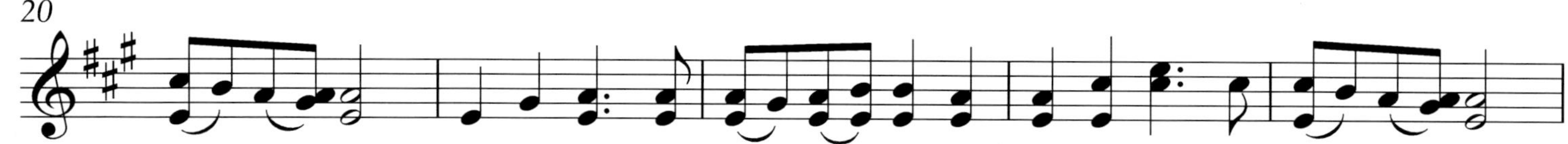

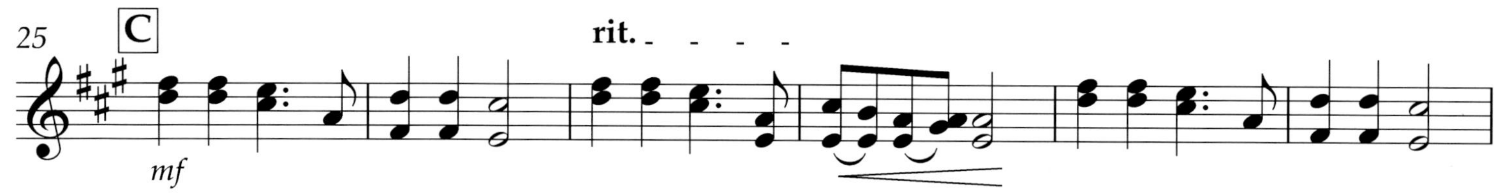

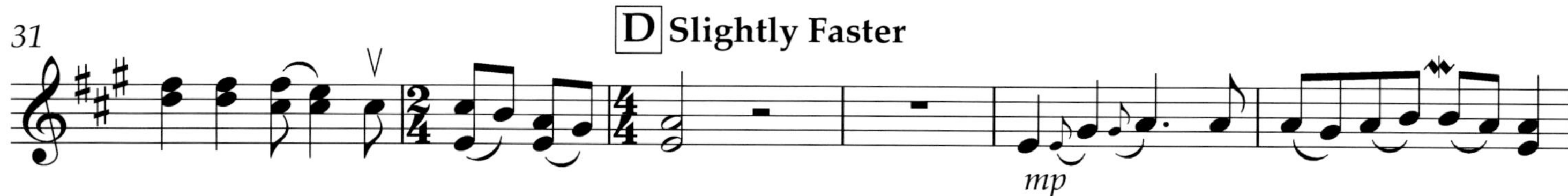

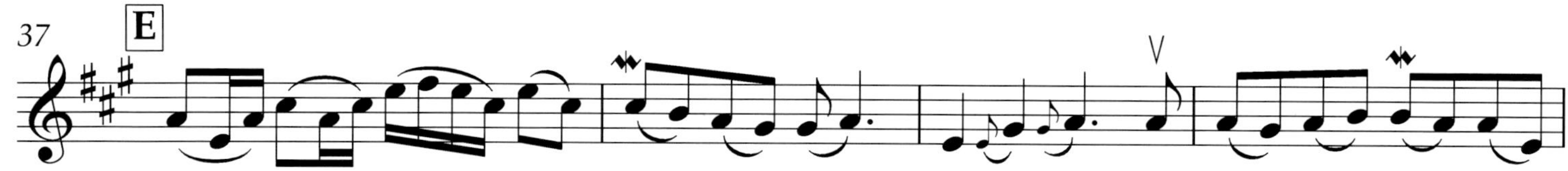

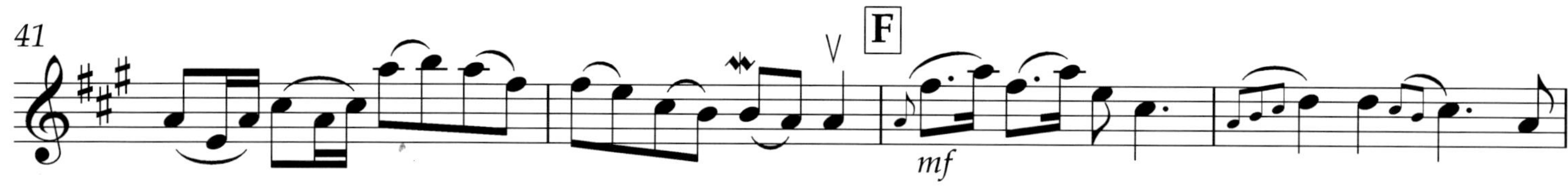

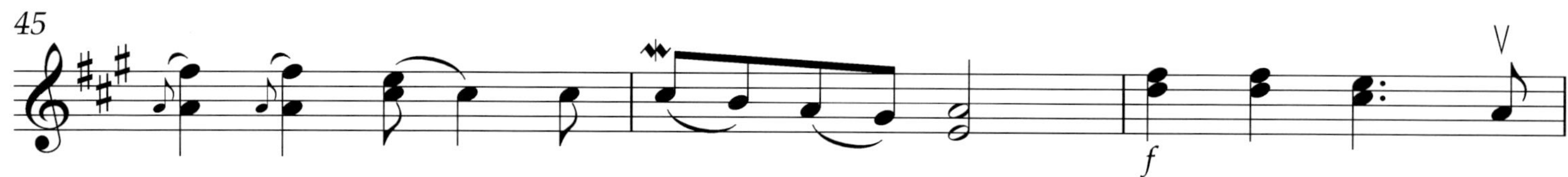

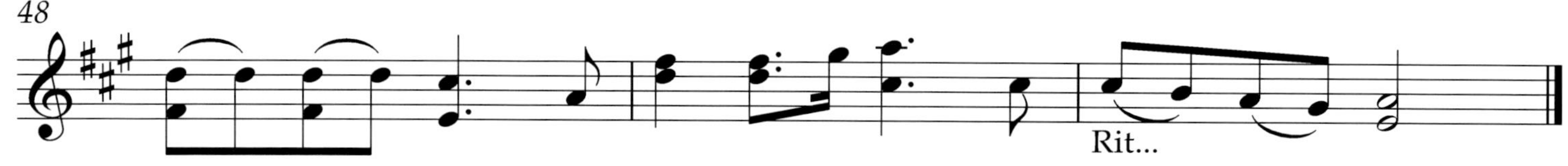

11

We Wish You a Merry Christmas

Traditional English
Arranged by The Wires: Sascha Groschang and Laurel Parks

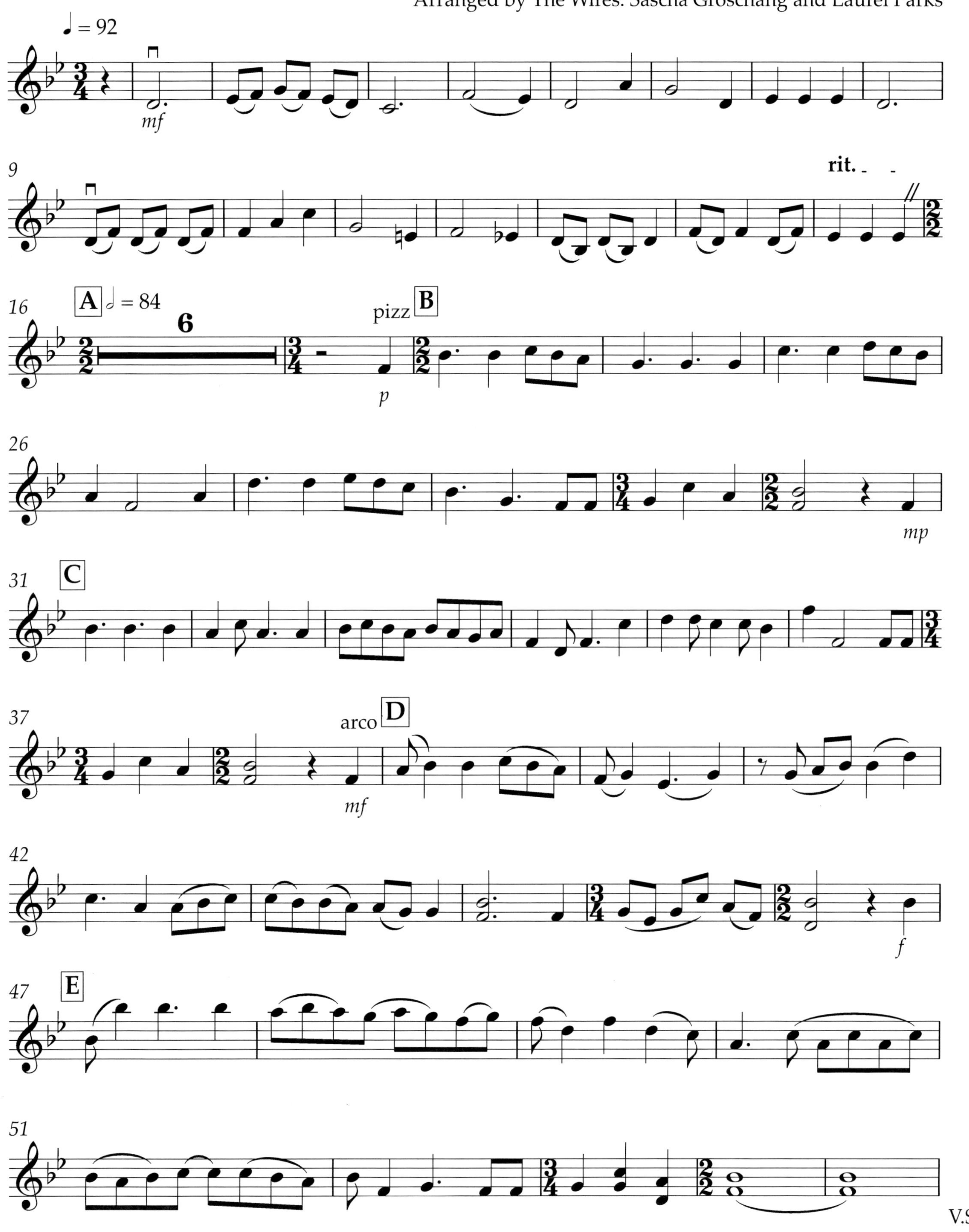

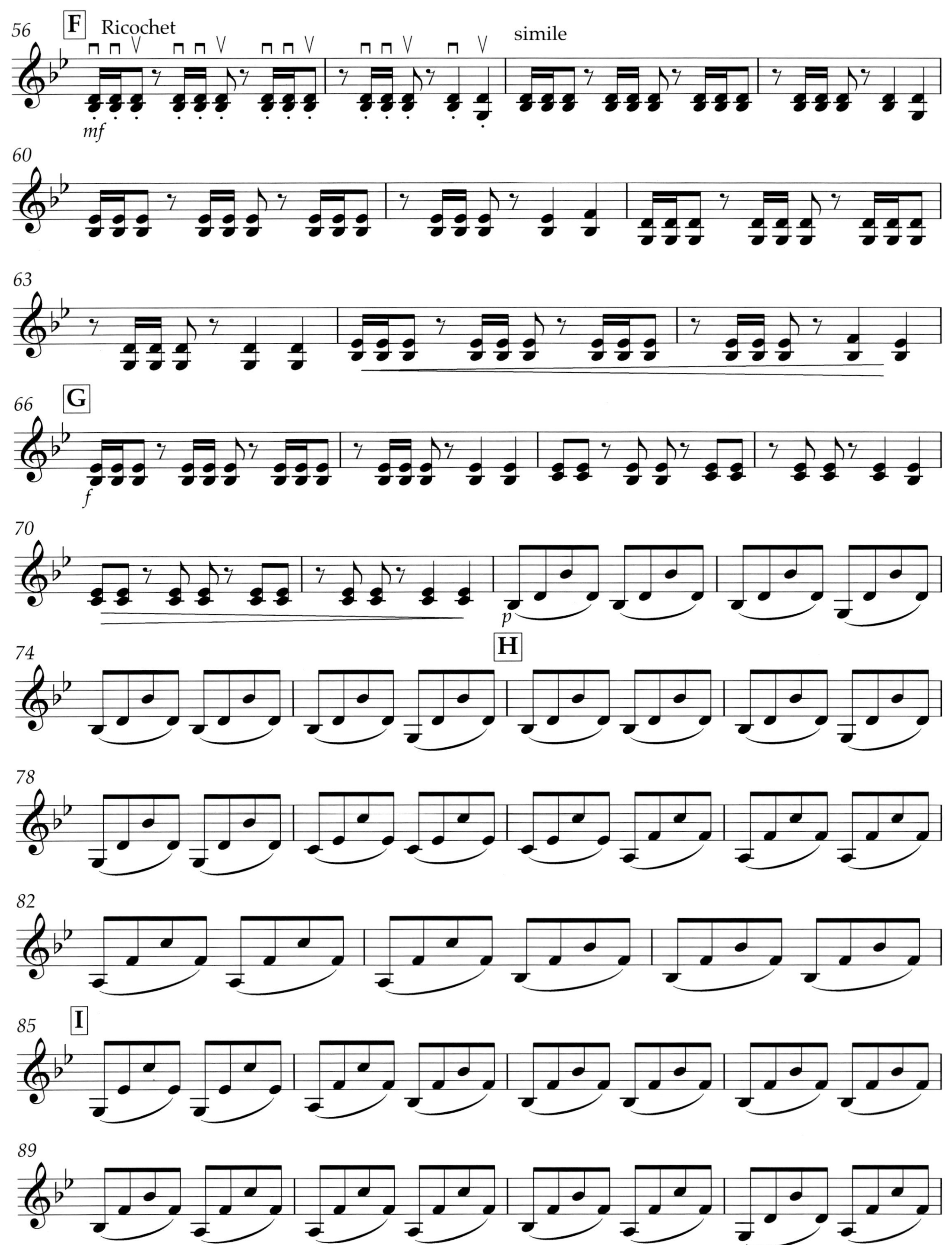
F
Ricochet
mf
simile
G
f
p
H
I

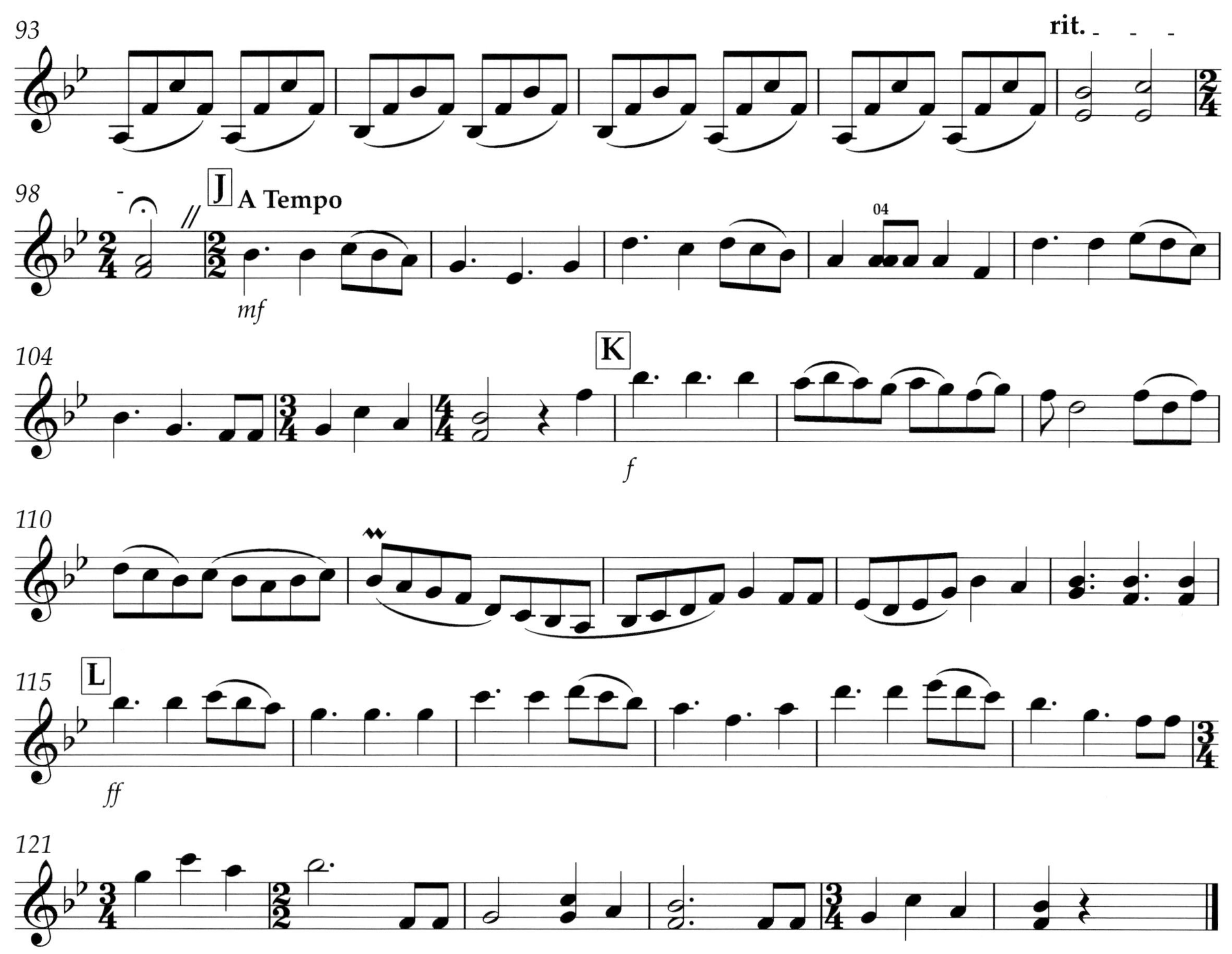
93
rit.
98
J
A Tempo
mf
04
104
K
f
110
115
L
ff
121

The Wires Duo

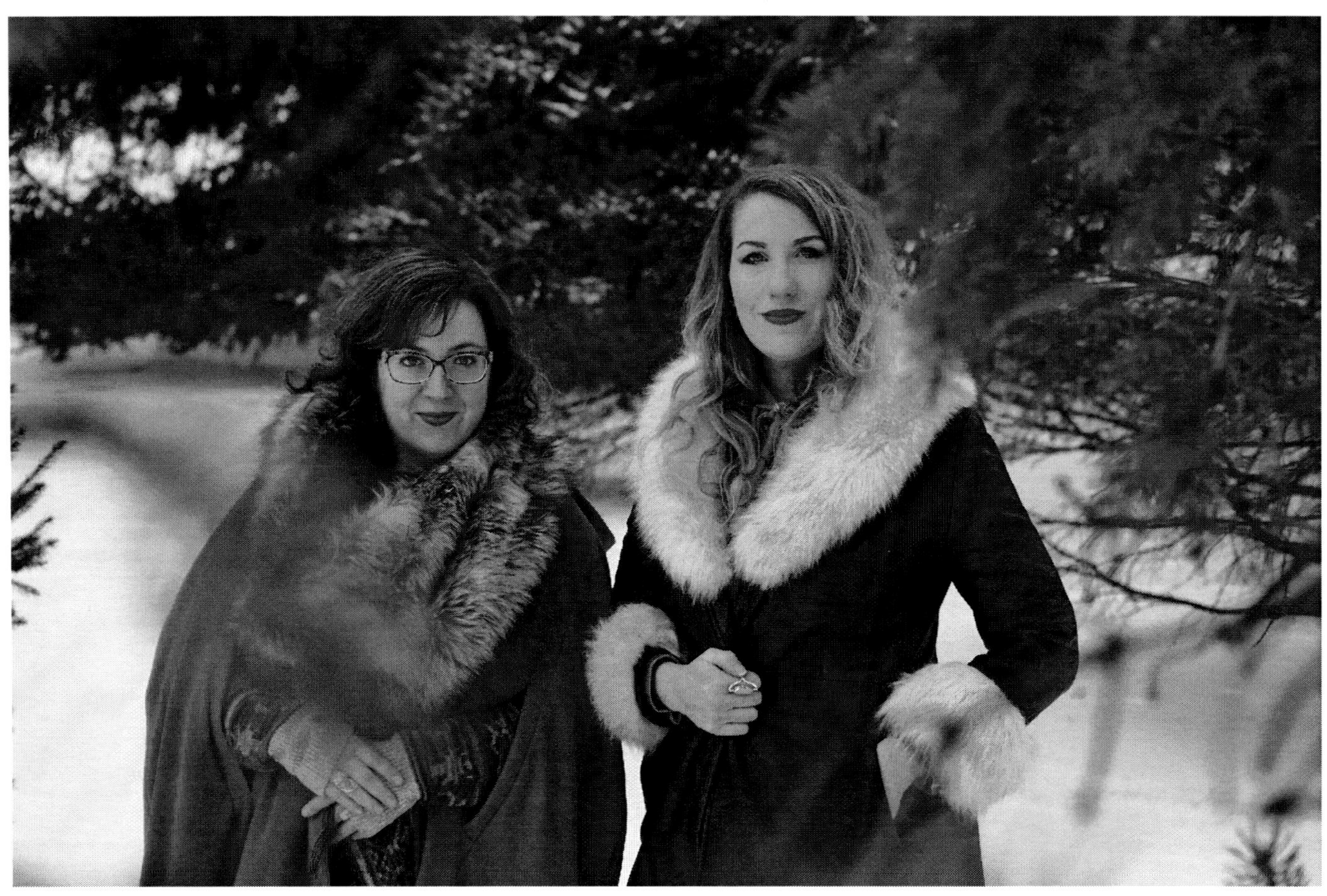

Sascha Groschang, Cello *Laurel Morgan Parks, Violin*

The Wires are a modern exploration in string sound. Created in Kansas City, Missouri, Laurel Morgan Parks, violin, and Sascha Groschang, cello, have been composing dynamic and cinematic music as best friends since 2009. Their music is inspired by imagery found in the natural world, folk styles, and modern string techniques. Following their debut album in 2012, their album "Wilder" (May 2019) is an imagined journey that includes depths of the oceanic world, the vast expanse of Celtic hills, the coldness of the frozen tundra and a discovery of the cosmos. Their holiday album, "Winter" (December 2020) encompasses cinematic, yet an intimate timbre, with the classic sounds of the season. The duo performs at festivals, concert halls, and music venues in the Midwest and beyond. Their online school, "Fiddle Life," (www. fiddlelife.com), teaches adults traditional styles at beginner and intermediate levels.

Other Mel Bay Violin Books

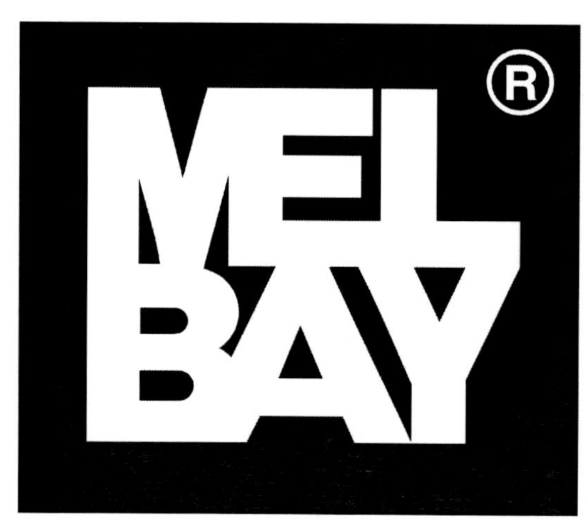
MEL BAY

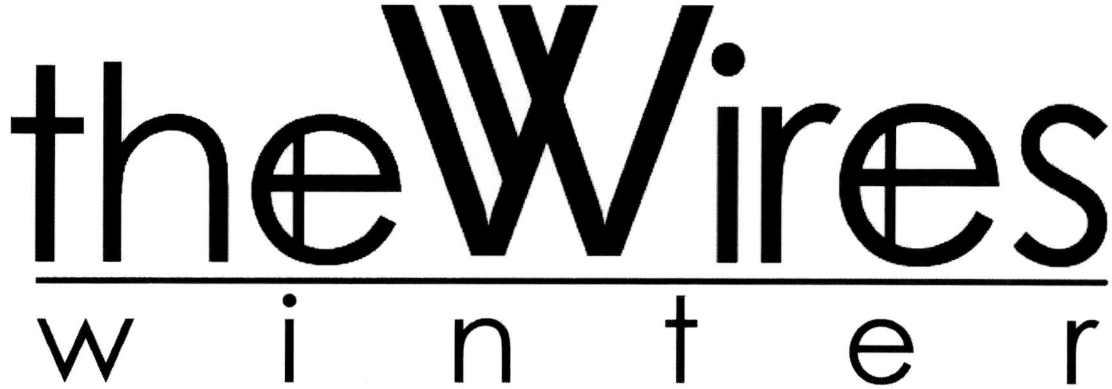

Folk Carols for Violin and Cello

Laurel Parks and Sascha Groschang

CELLO PART

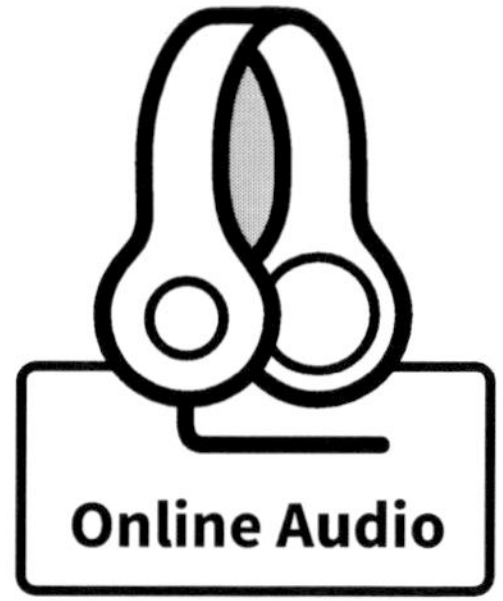

To access the online audio recording by The Wires Duo go to:
WWW.MELBAY.COM/31037MEB

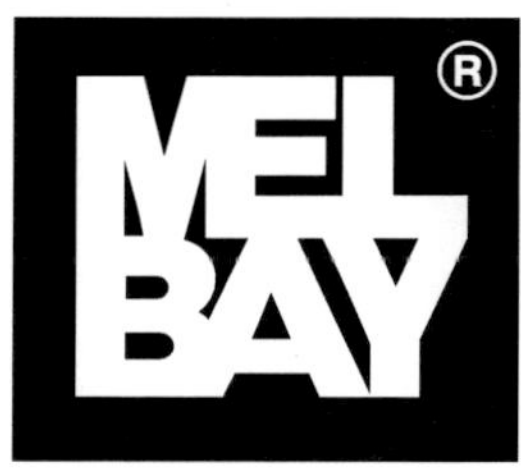

WWW.MELBAY.COM

Contents

Performance Notes

We've notated many of the ornaments heard on our studio recording "Winter." However, all of these pieces are inspired by folk idioms. Feel free to take away or add your own ornaments, slides and double stops. This music is less rigid than traditional classical music so there is plenty of room for micro-improvisations. In other words, make these pieces your own!

A few specific techniques are used in the cello parts. Several of the tunes use the chopping technique. This technique is indicated by an 'X' notehead. *Greensleeves* and *We Wish You a Merry Christmas* use a strumming pizzicato technique and *We Wish You a Merry Christmas* uses a fingerboard slap, as indicated with a slash notehead.

The chop utilizes a straight thumb and is a combination of dropping the bow heavily on the string and allowing the bow to scrape the strings. Your bow hair will be angled slightly towards the floor, and your contact point will be closer to the bridge than usual. The note after the chop will be a quasi-chop. The act of releasing the bow off the string will create a sort of ghost note, a little bit of pitch will be heard, and a small chopping scrape sound will also be audible.

For the strumming technique, you will use your thumb to pizzicato on the lower strings, away from your body. For the top strings, you will use your 3rd finger to pluck toward your body. For the slap pizzicato technique, you'll slap your fingerboard, allowing the strings to hit the wood to create a nice percussive sound. For each of these techniques, the most important thing is that the groove stays steady, so don't worry too much about perfection!

For video instructions on all 3 techniques: Find "TheWiresDuo" channel on Youtube and search for the "Special Cello Techniques" video: https://www.youtube.com/watch?v=oc34FkDRI_U

Lo, How a Rose E'er Blooming

1

Michael Praetorius
Arranged by The Wires: Sascha Groschang and Laurel Parks

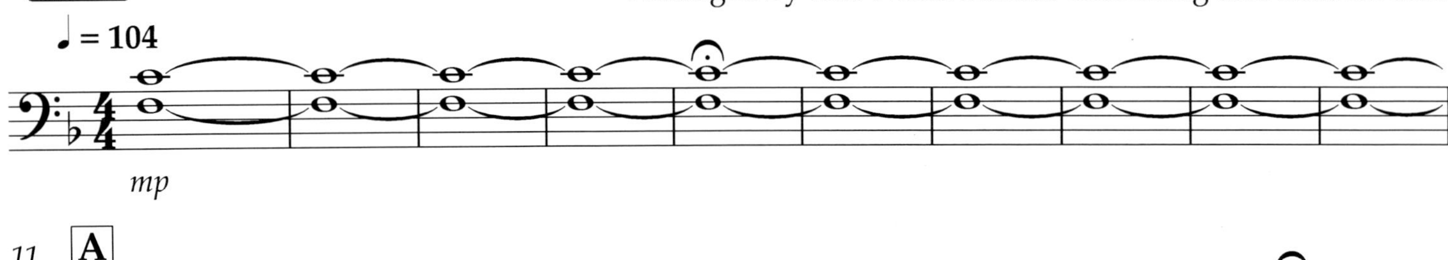

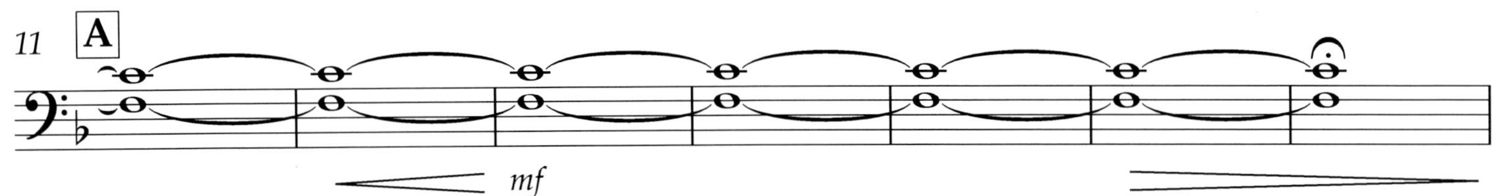

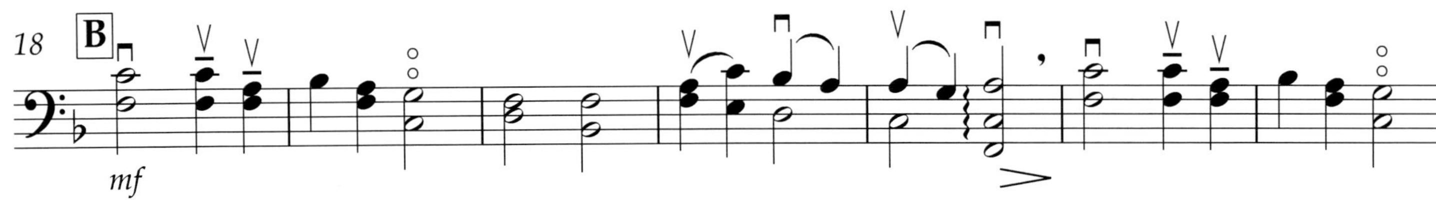

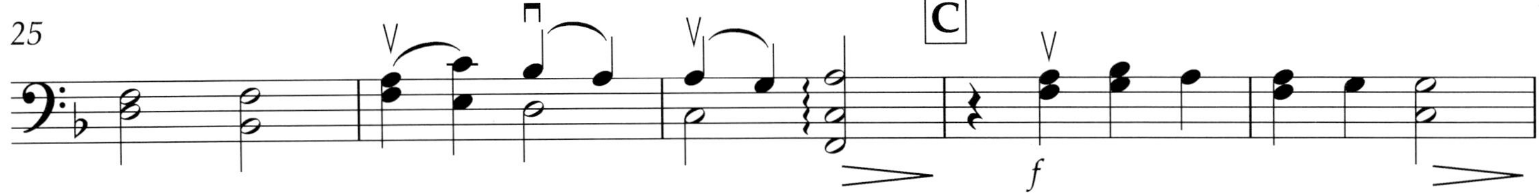

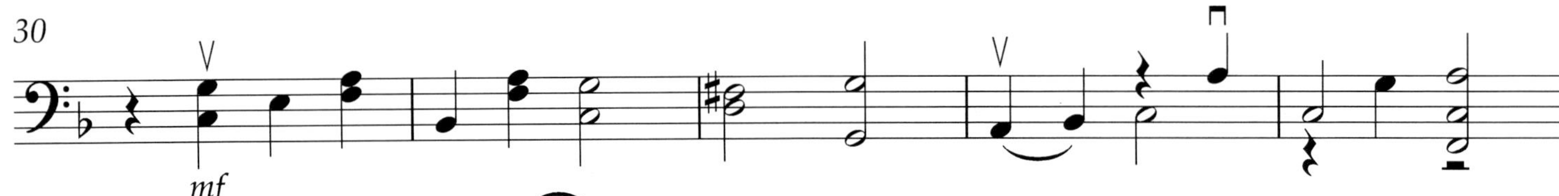

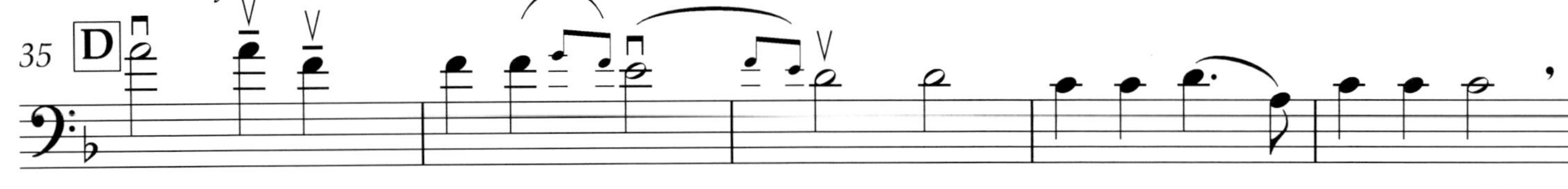

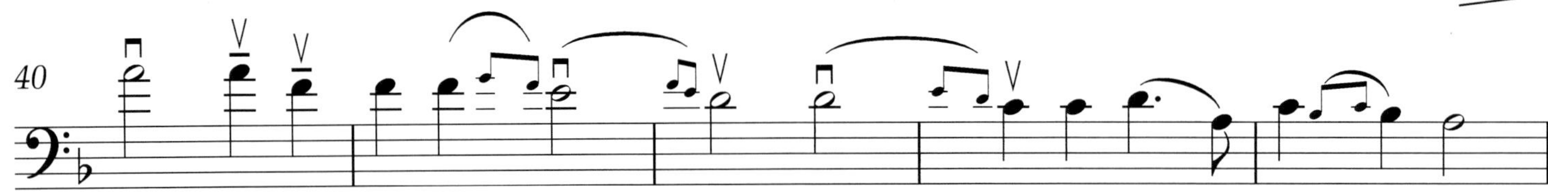

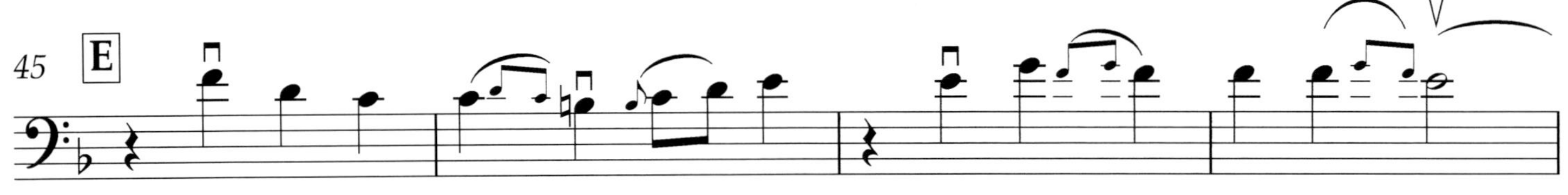

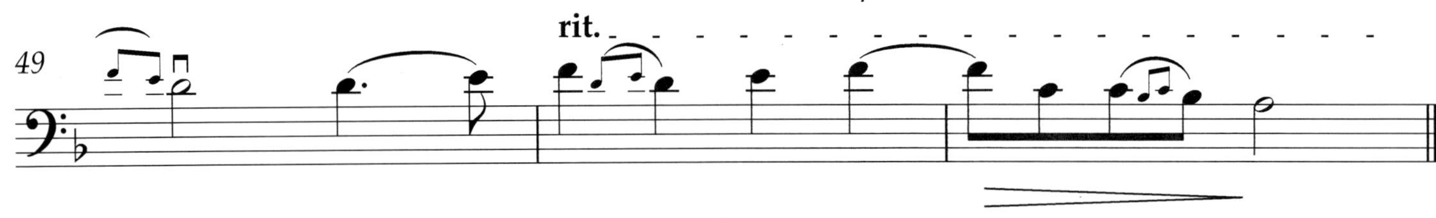

2
Coventry Carol
Traditional
Arranged by The Wires: Sascha Groschang and Laurel Parks
Freely
ff
tr
7
A
pizz ♩ = 104
p
13
18
23
B
29
35
rit.
C
Faster ♩ = 172
arco
f
42
3
48
D

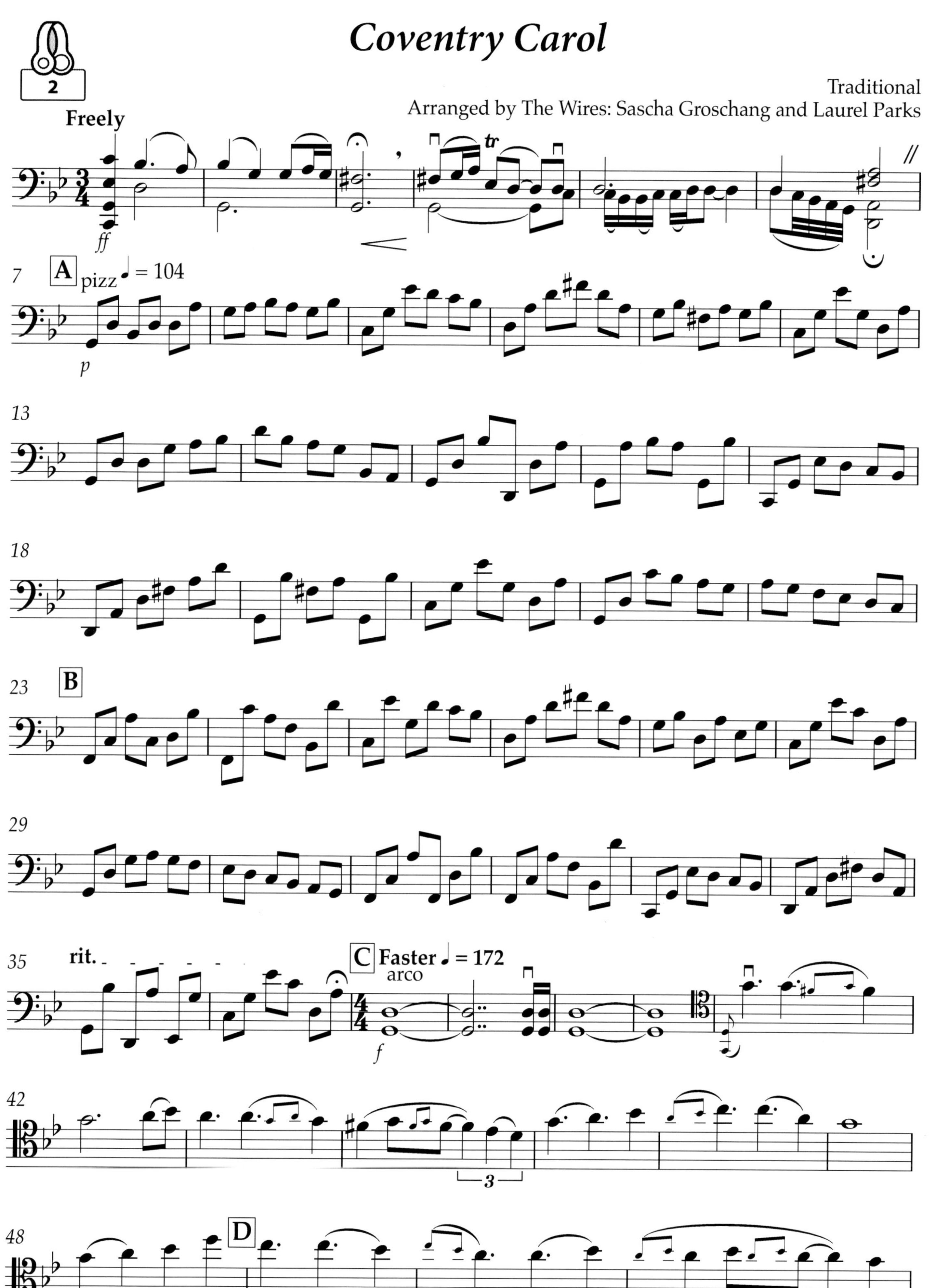

V.S.

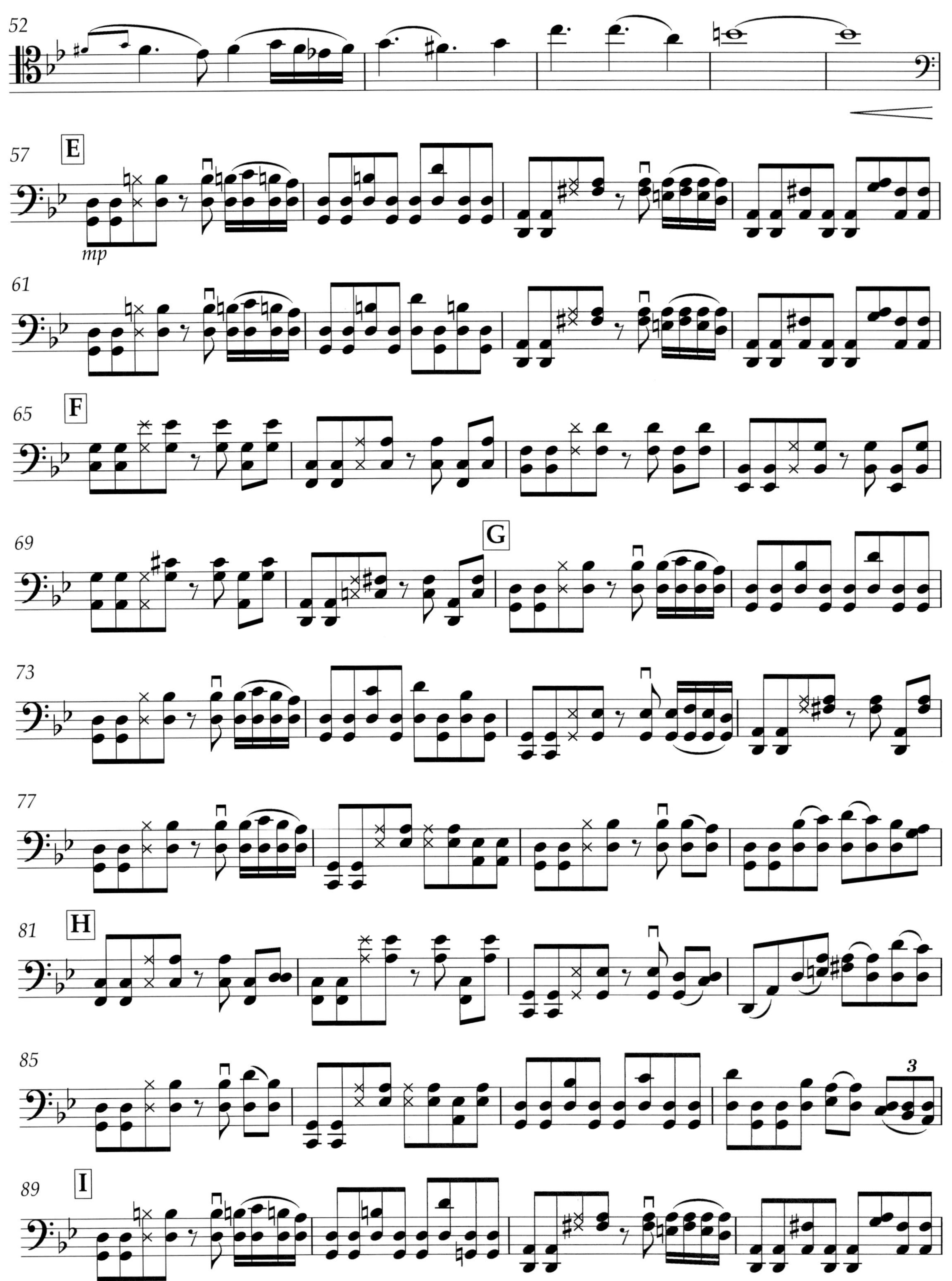
52
57
E
mp
61
65
F
69
G
73
77
81
H
85
3
89
I

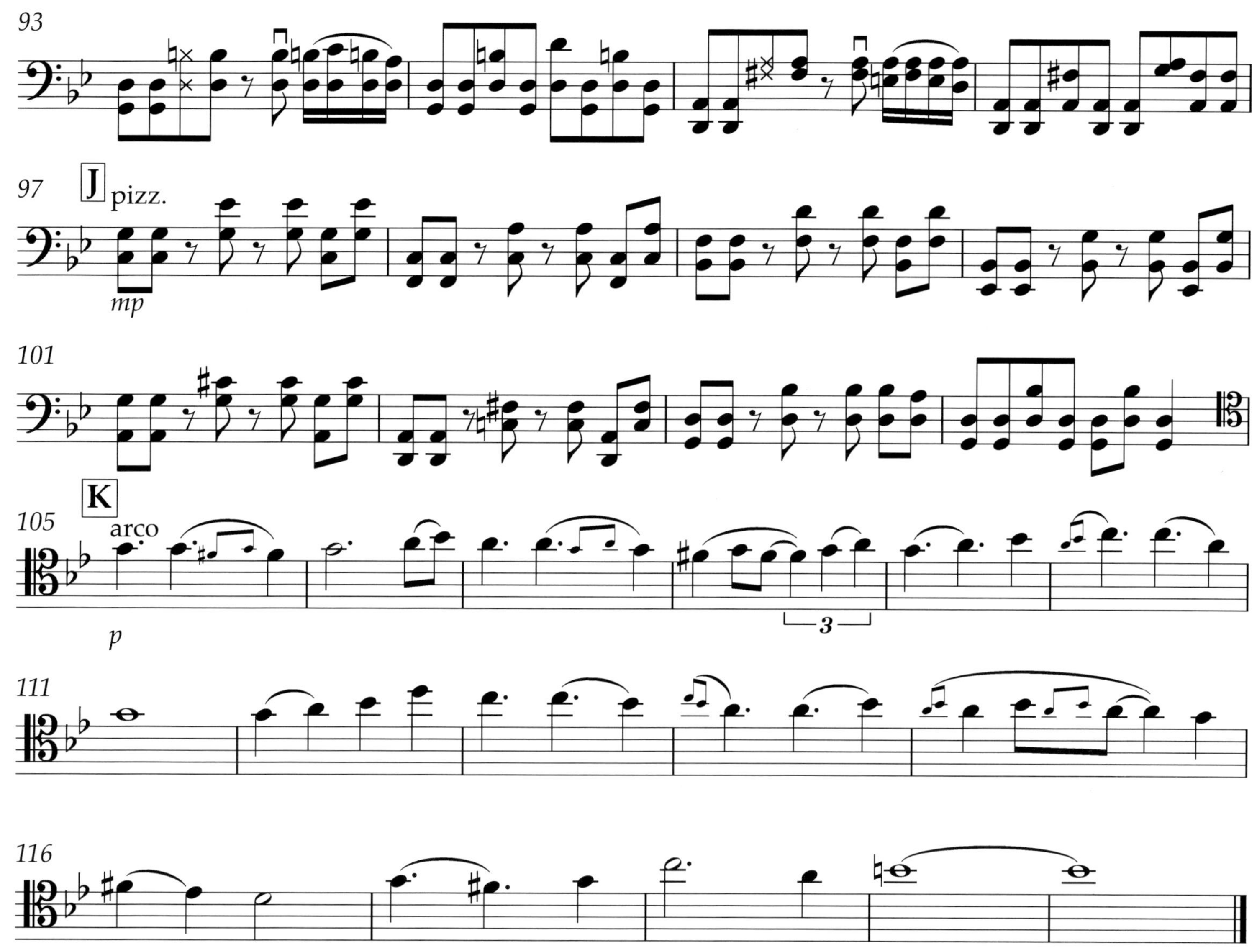
93
97
J
pizz.
mp
101
105
K
arco
p
3
111
116

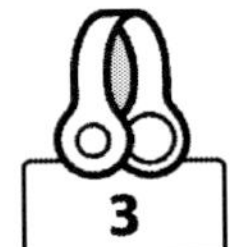

Silent Night

Franz Xaver Gruber
Arranged by The Wires: Sascha Groschang and Laurel Parks

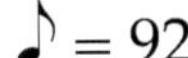

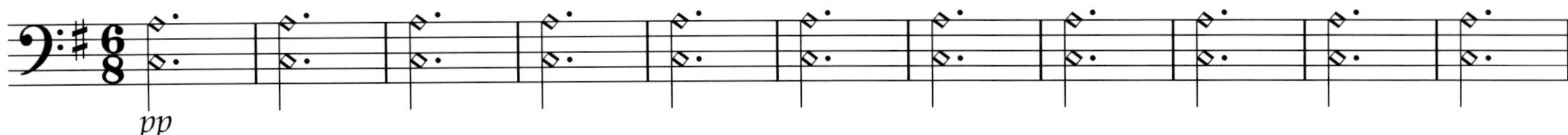

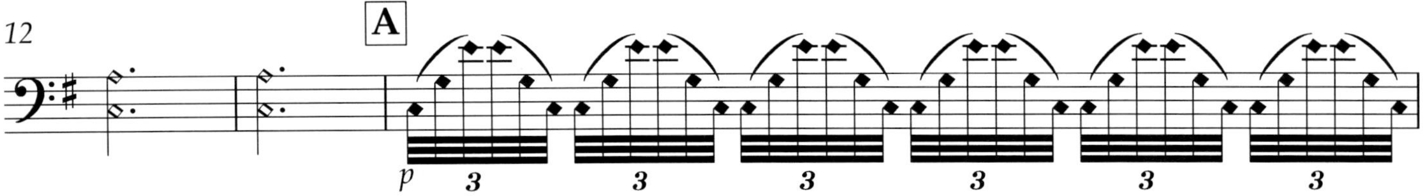

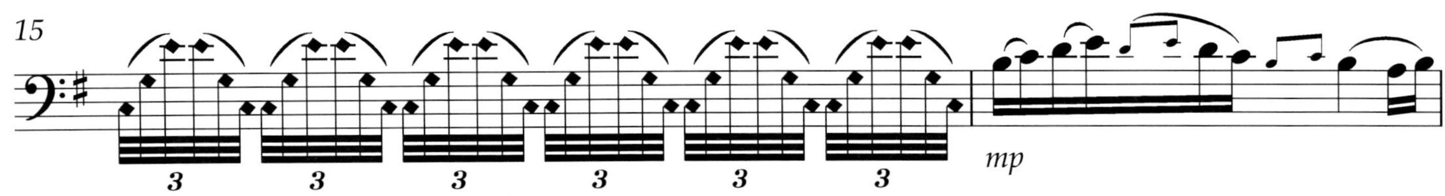

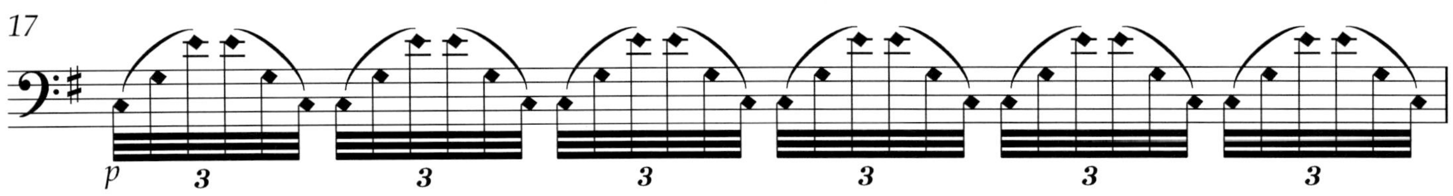

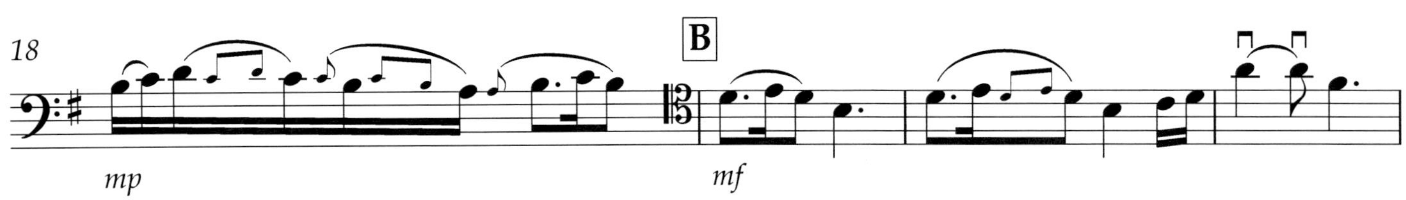

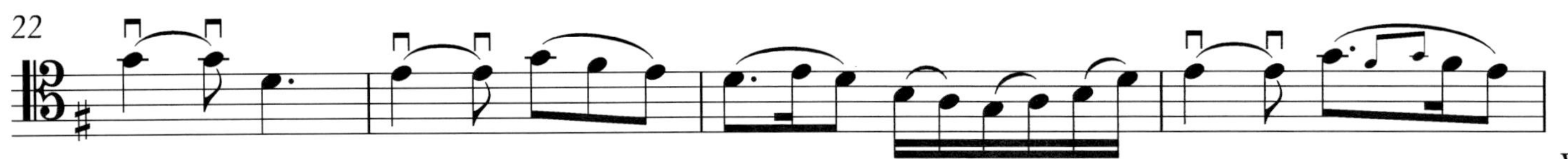

V.S.

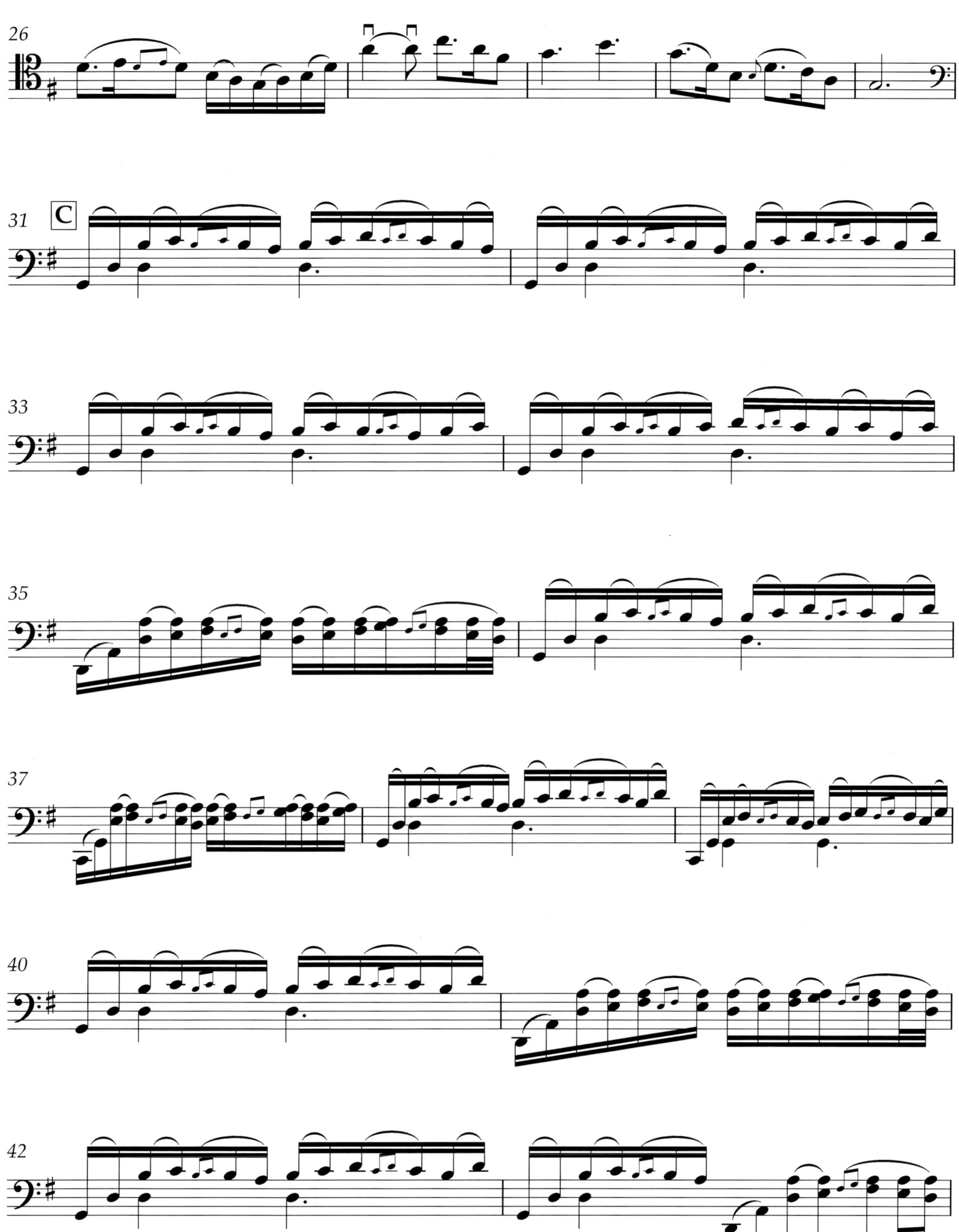
26
31
C
33
35
37
40
42

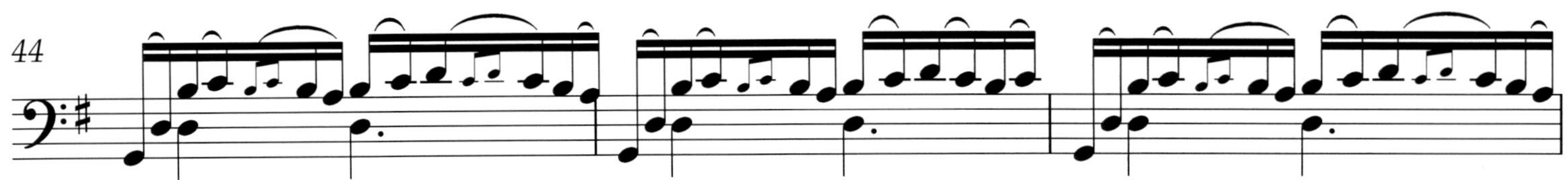
44
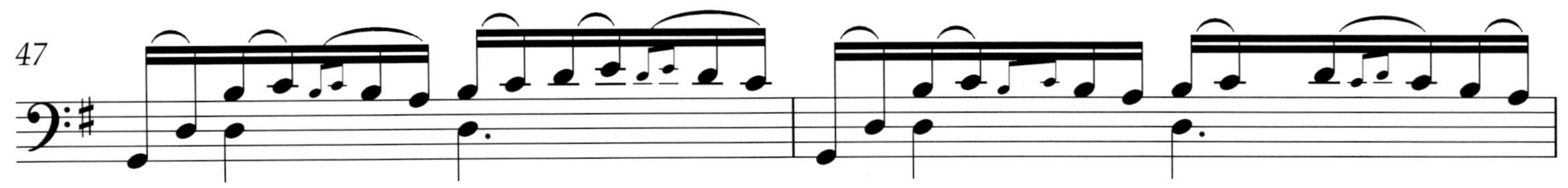
47
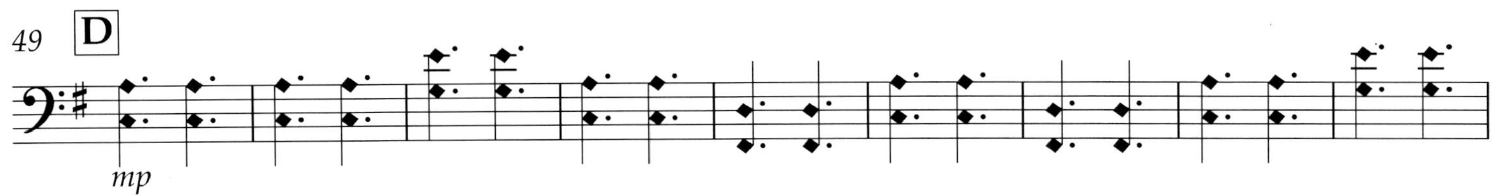
49
D
mp
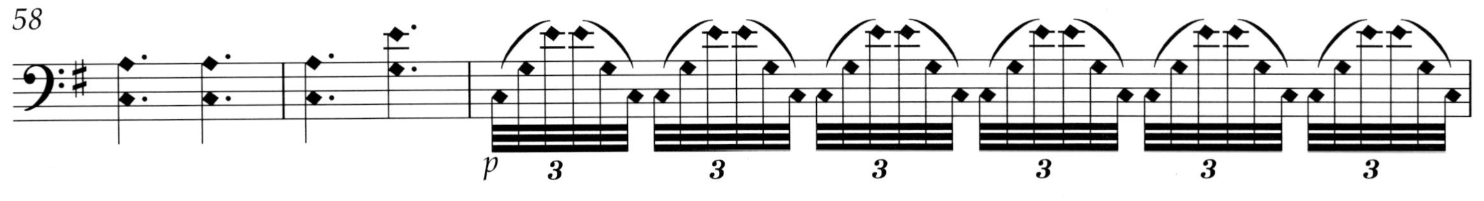
58
p
3
3
3
3
3
3
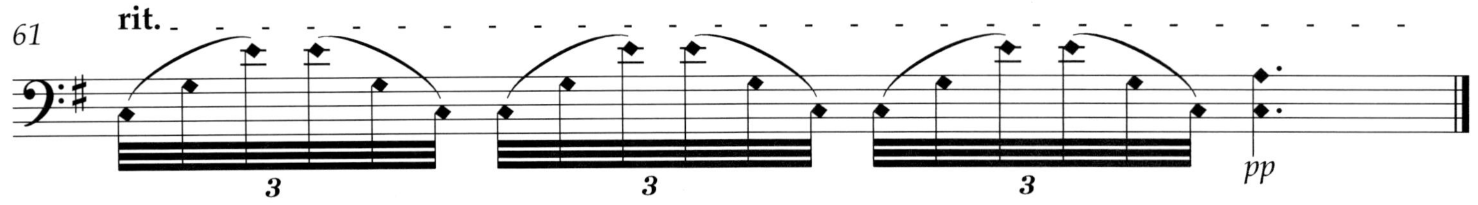
61
rit.
3
3
3
pp

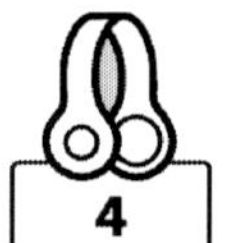

Greensleeves

Traditional
Arranged by The Wires: Sascha Groschang and Laurel Parks

♪ = 132

mp

3 A

p

6 B

9

12

15 C

f

19

D

23 pizz.

mp

26

V.S.

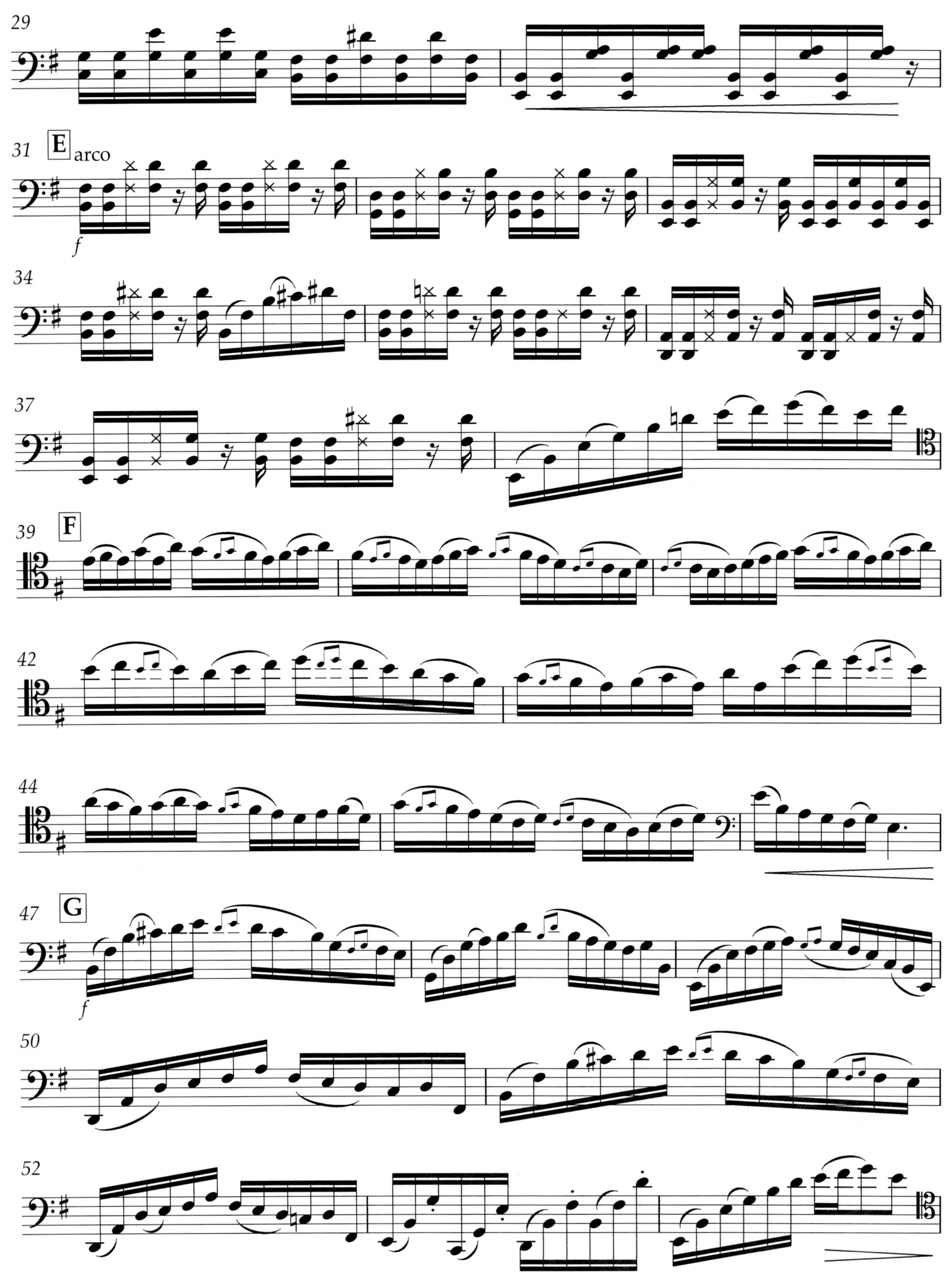
29
31
E
arco
f
34
37
39
F
42
44
47
G
f
50
52

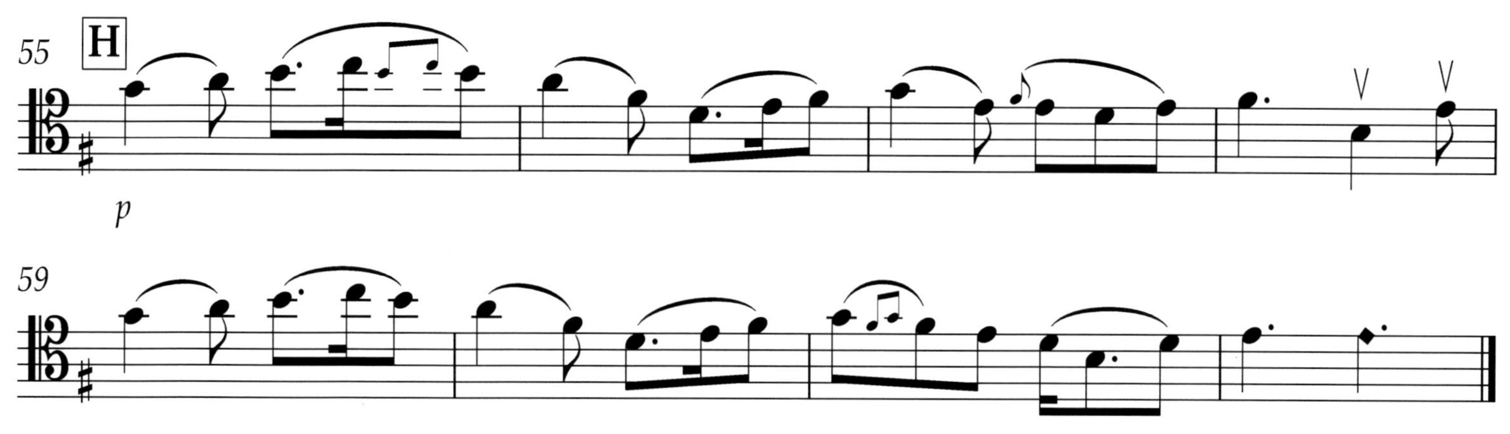
55
H
p
59

The Holly and the Ivy

Arranged by The Wires: Sascha Groschang and Laurel Parks

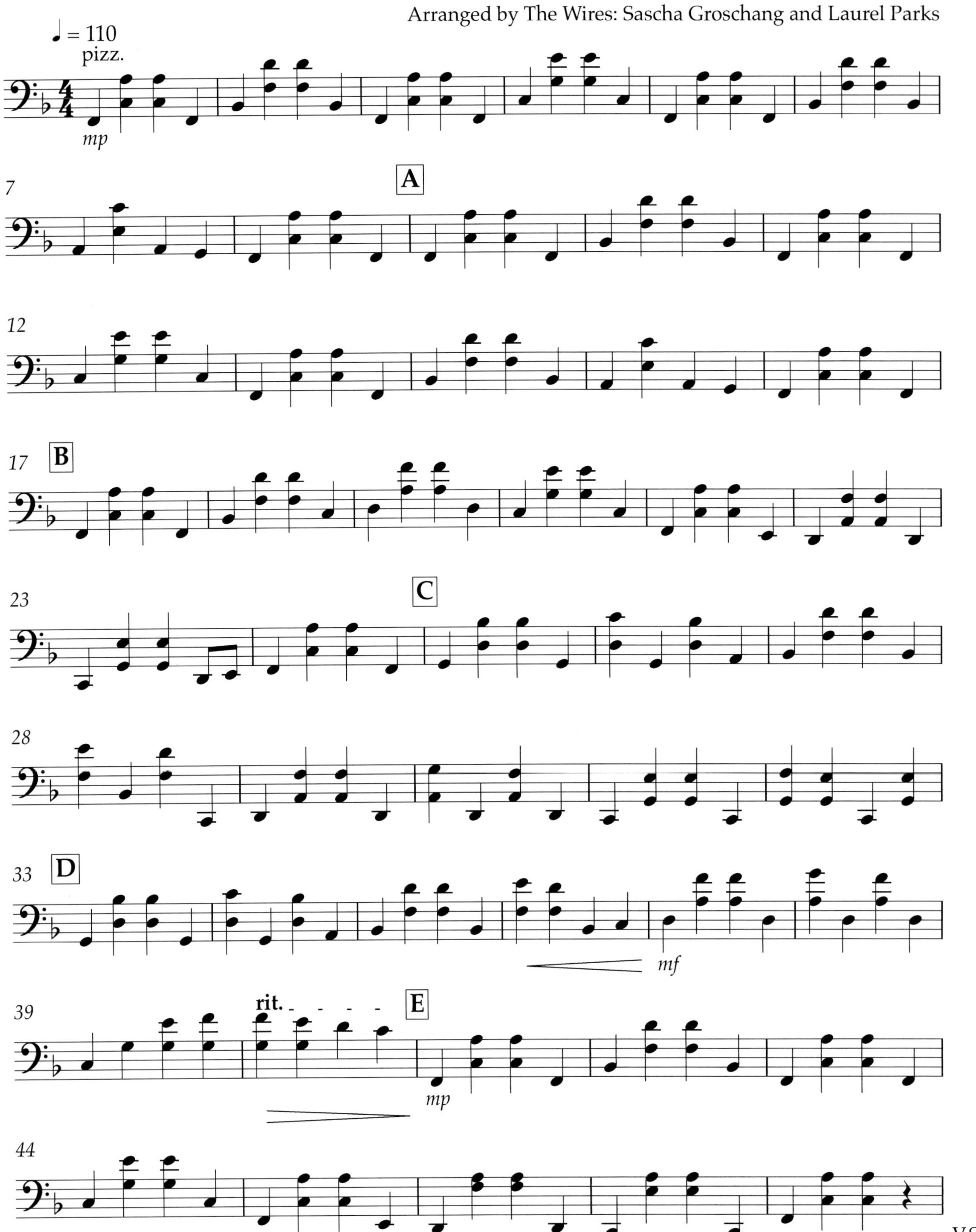

V.S.

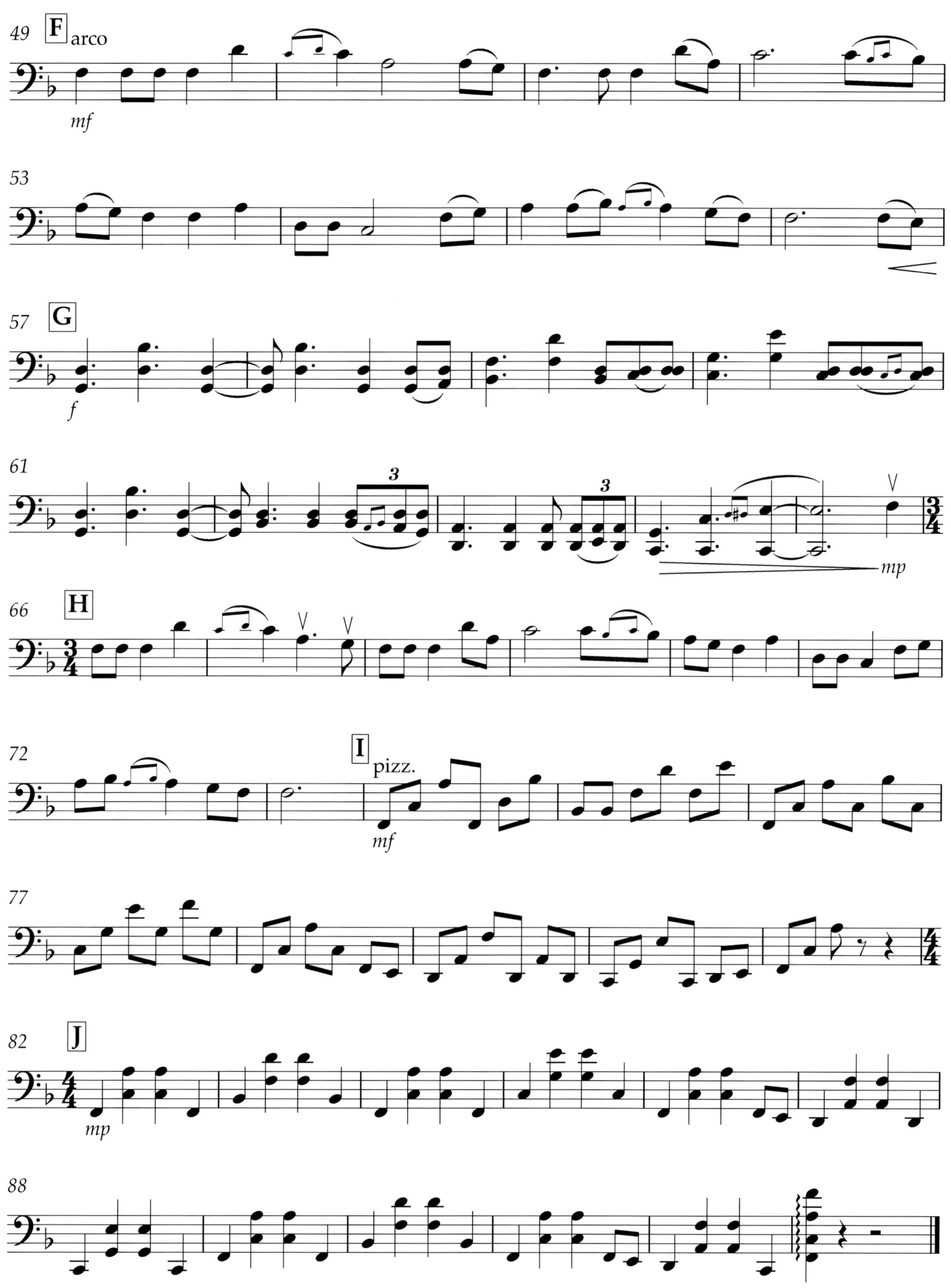
49
F
arco
mf
53
57
G
f
61
3
3
mp
66
H
72
I
pizz.
mf
77
82
J
mp
88

Wexford Carol

Tradtional English
Arranged by The Wires: Sascha Groschang and Laurel Parks

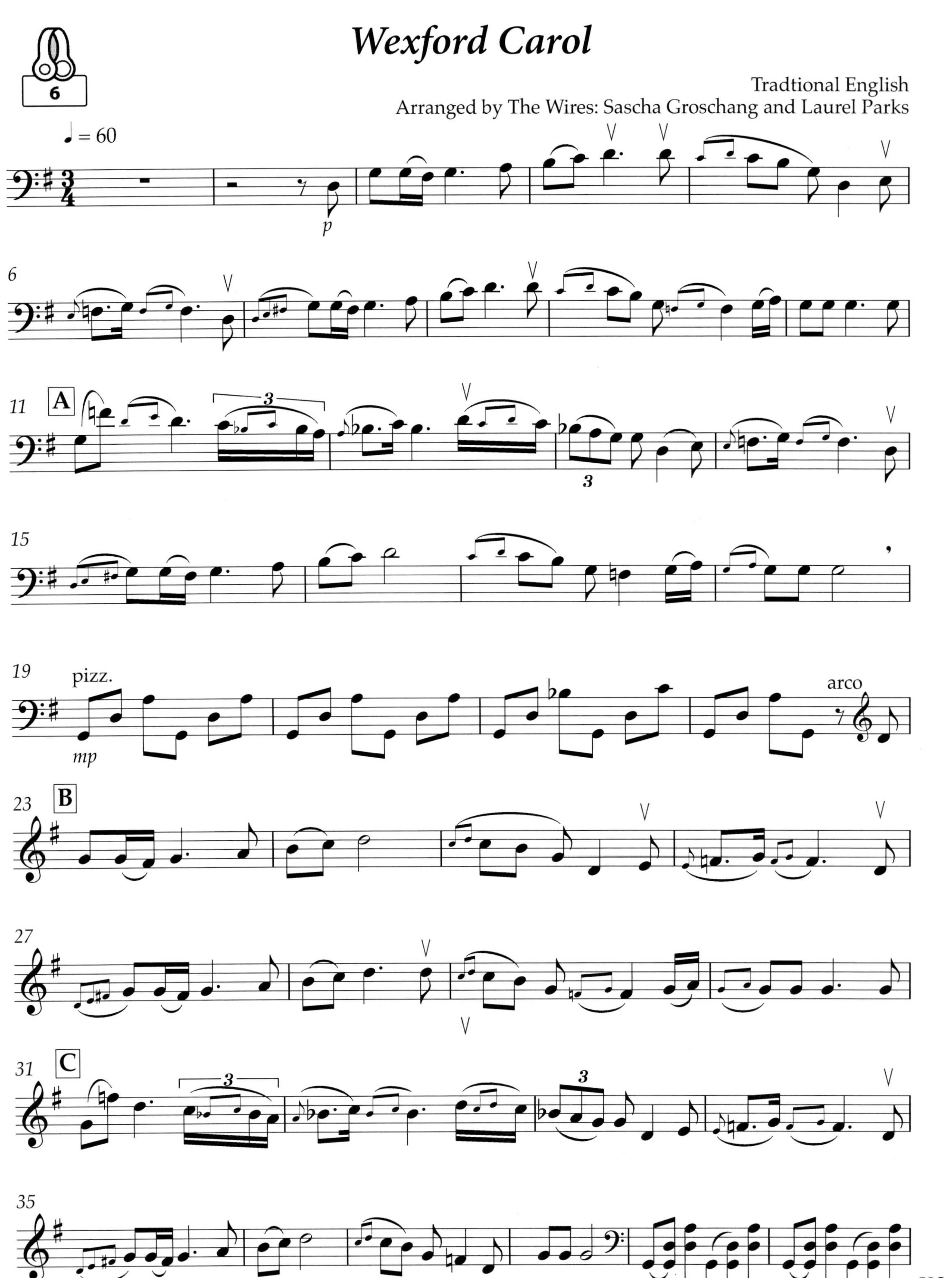

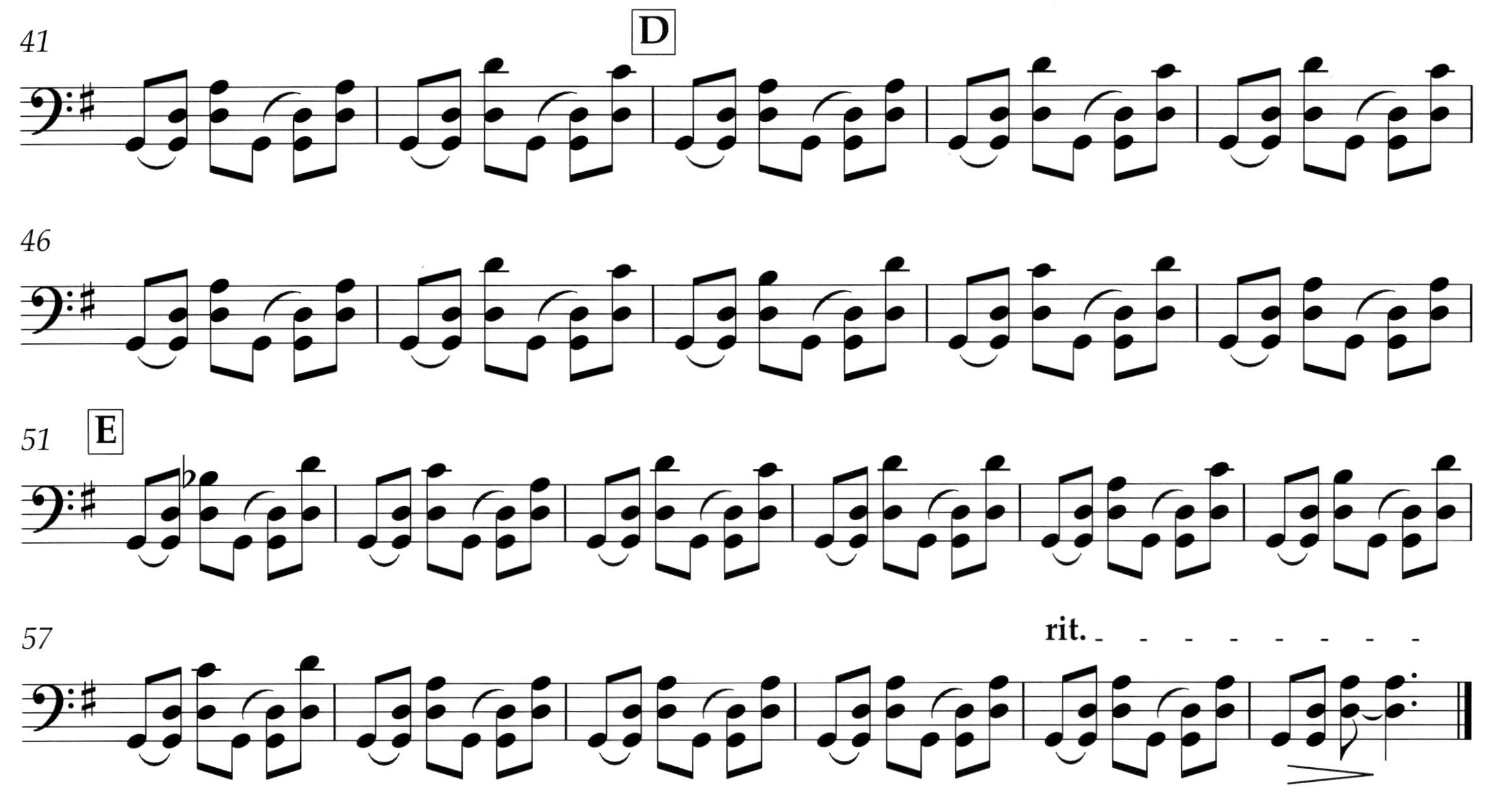
41
D
46
51
E
57
rit.

Bring a Torch Jeannette, Isabella

Traditional French
Arranged by the Wires: Sascha Groschang and Laurel Parks

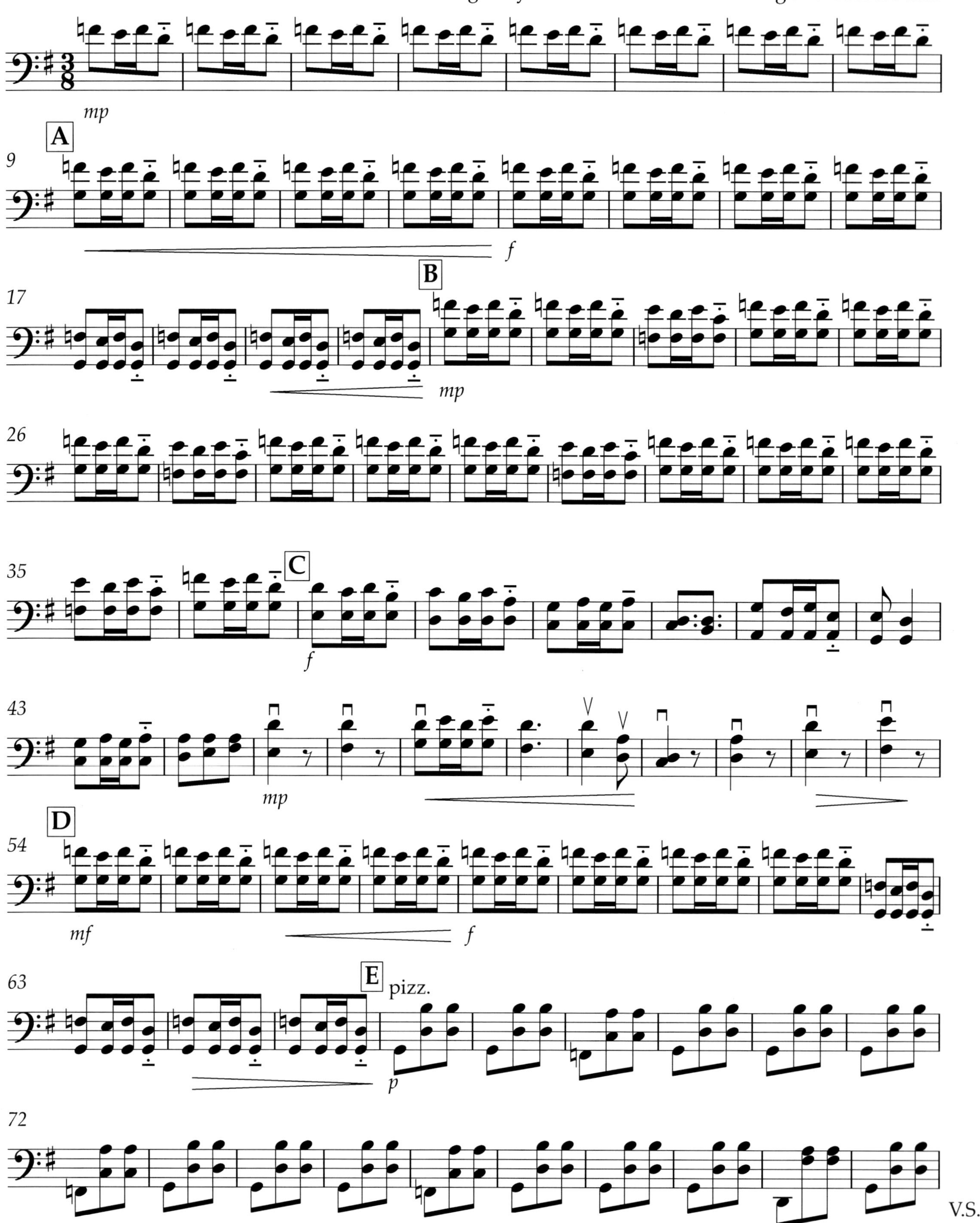

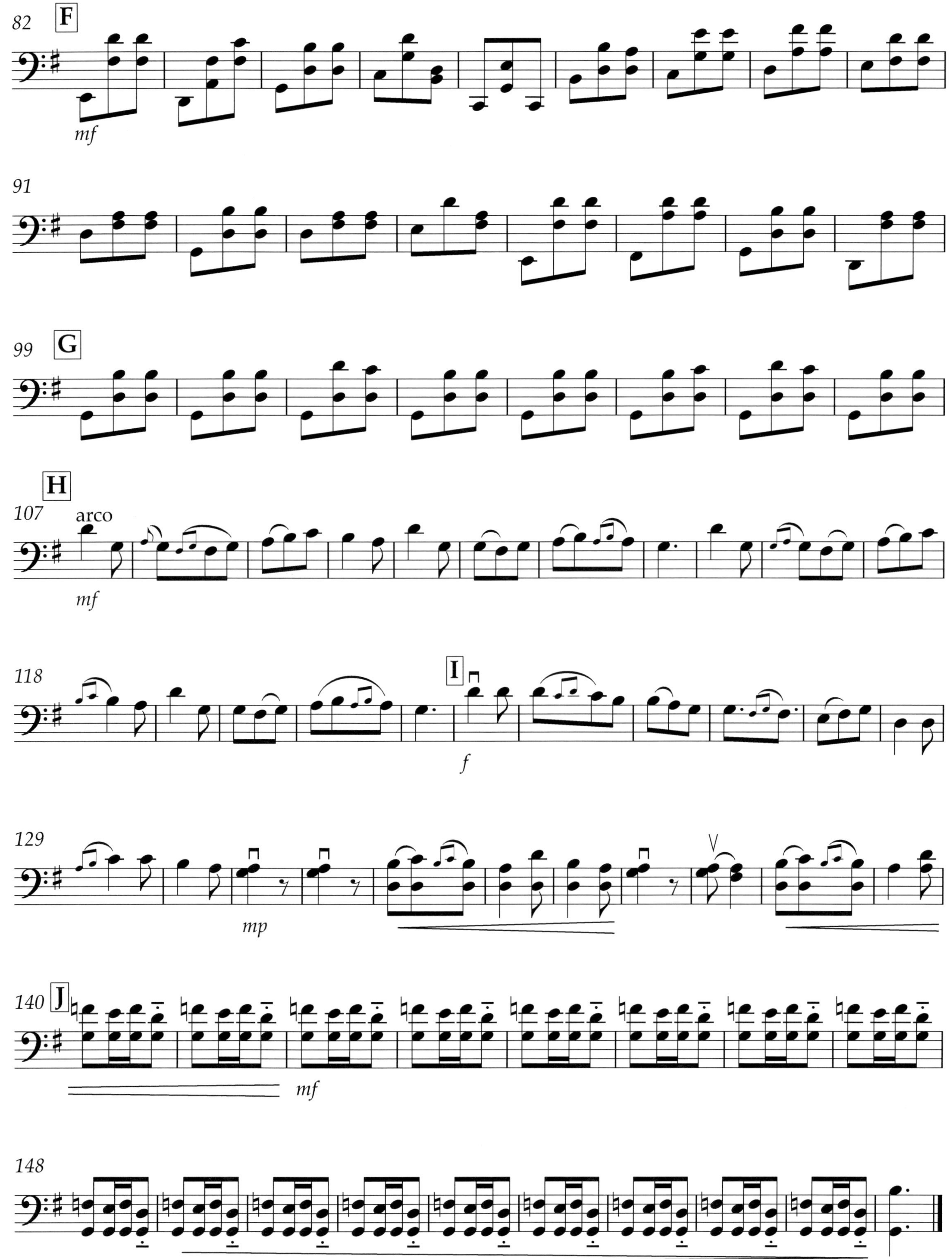
82
F
mf
91
99
G
H
107
arco
mf
118
I
f
129
mp
140
J
mf
148

In the Bleak Midwinter

Gustav Holst
Arranged by The Wires: Sascha Groschang and Laurel Parks

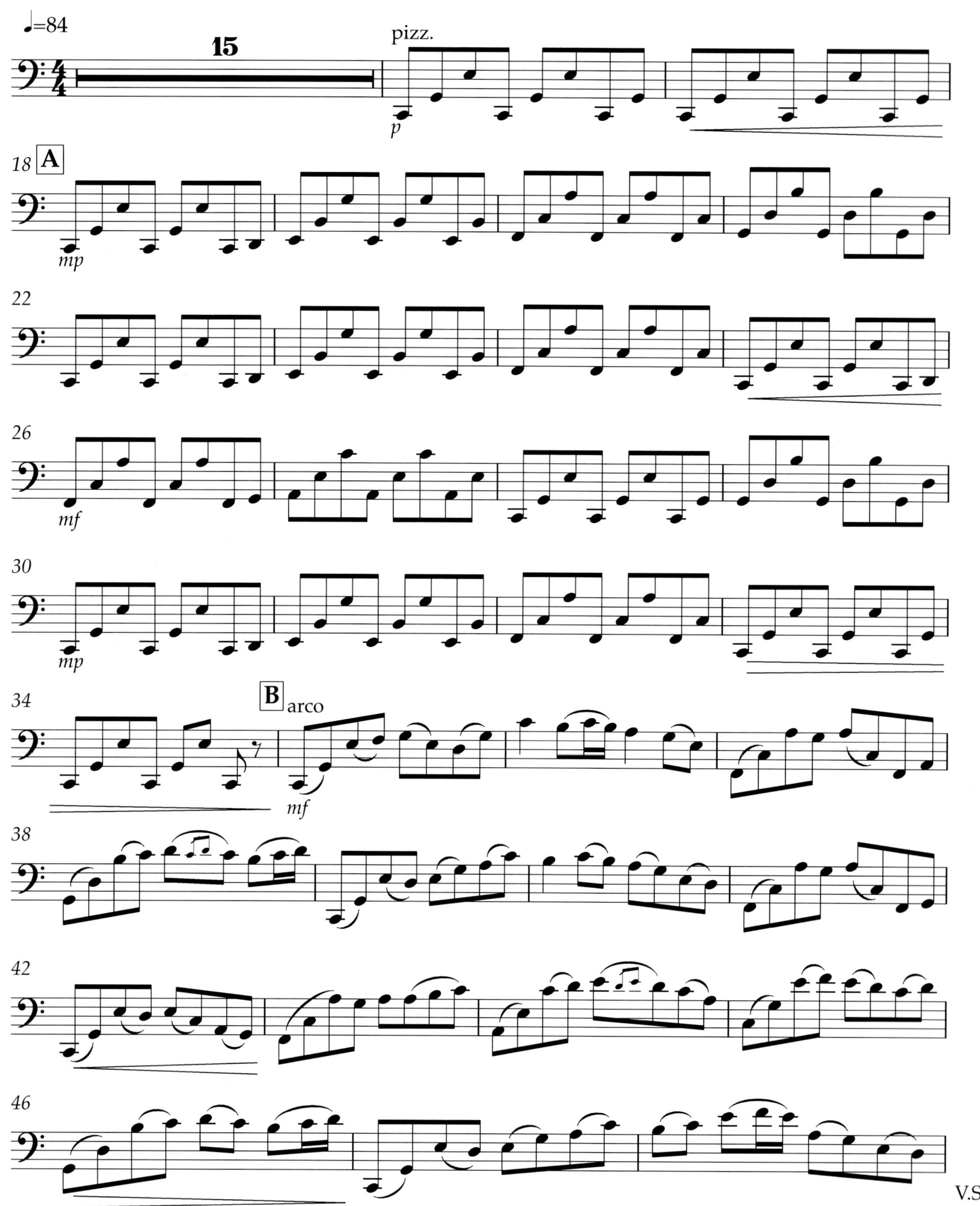

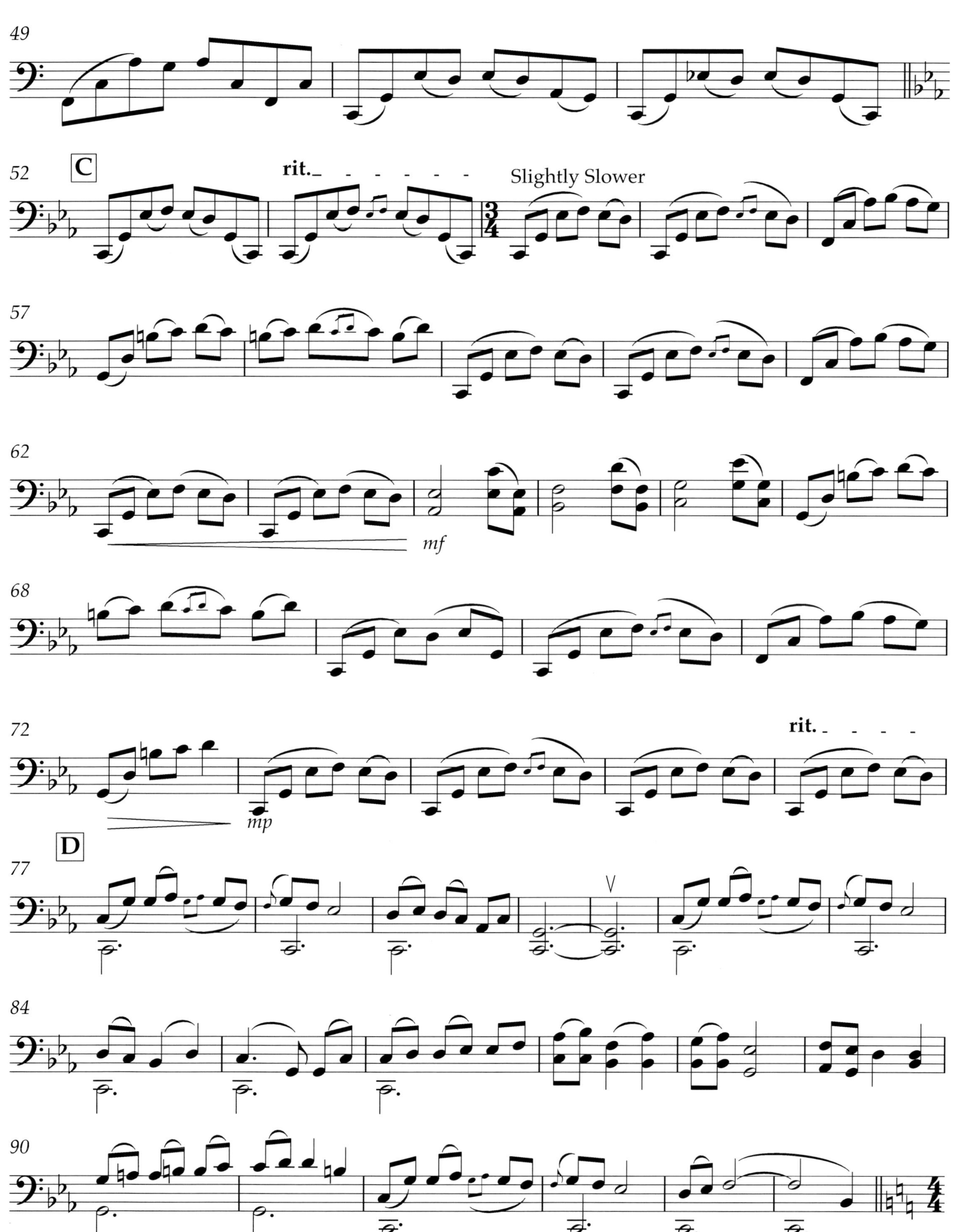

49
52
C
rit.
Slightly Slower
57
62
mf
68
72
mp
rit.
D
77
84
90

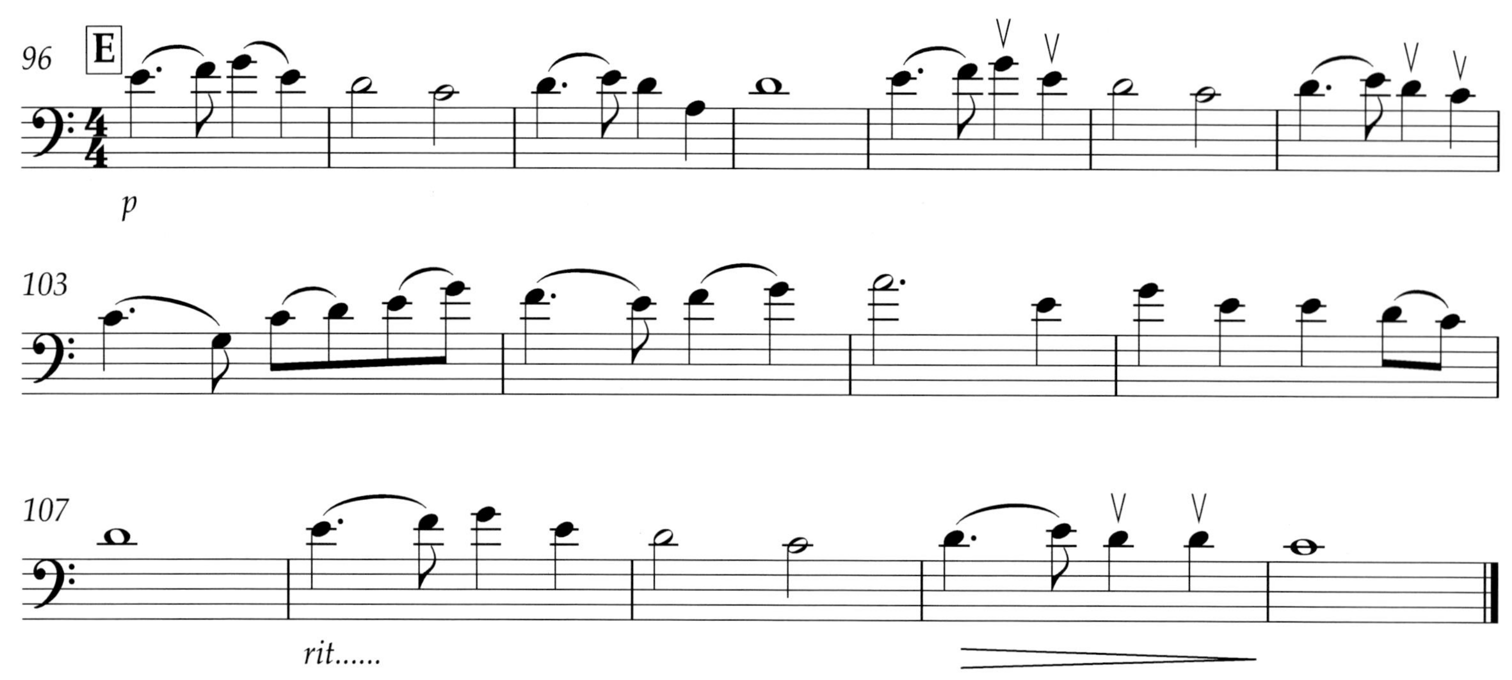
96
E
p
103
107
rit......

This page has been left blank to avoid an awkward page turn.

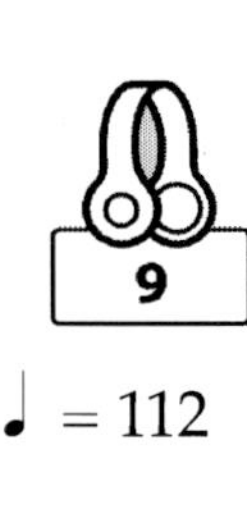

Campbell Street

The Wires: Sascha Groschang and Laurel Parks

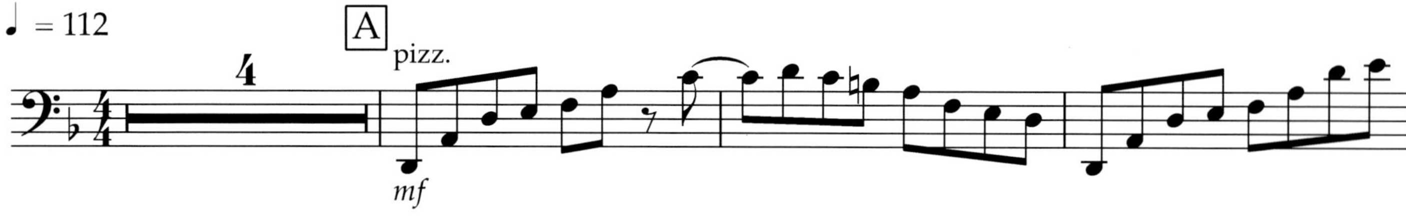

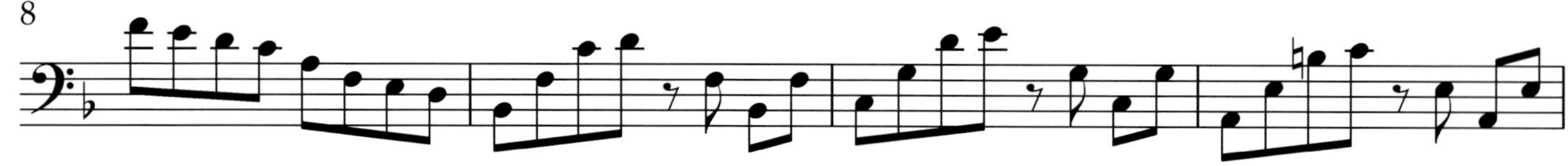

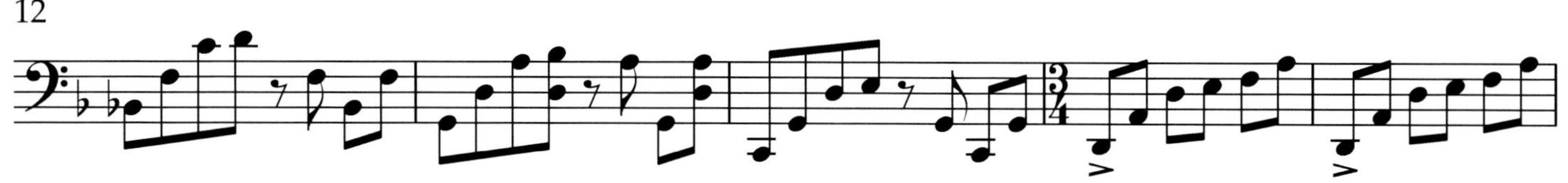

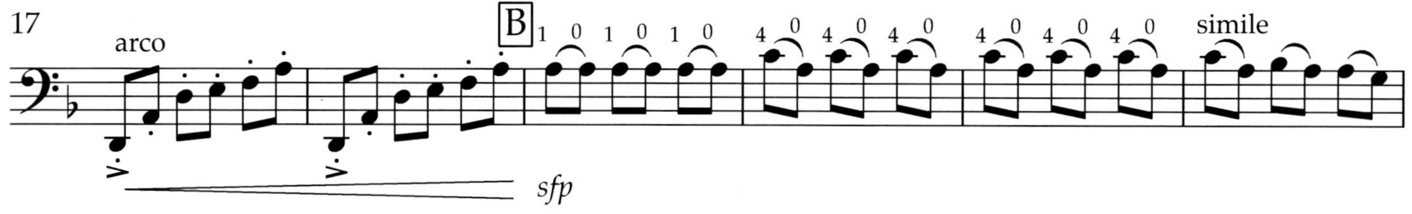

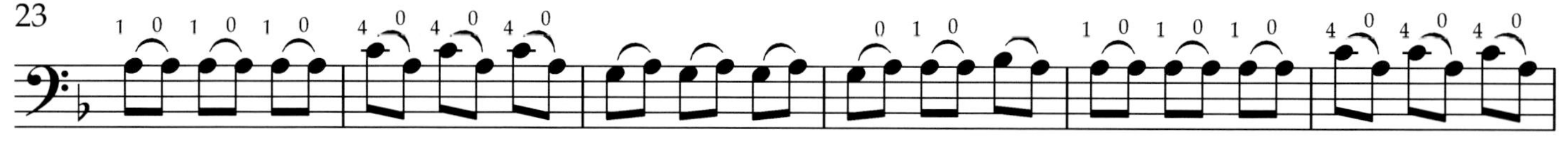

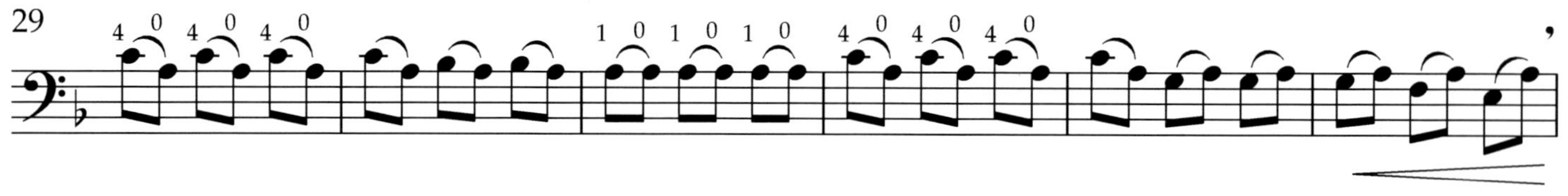

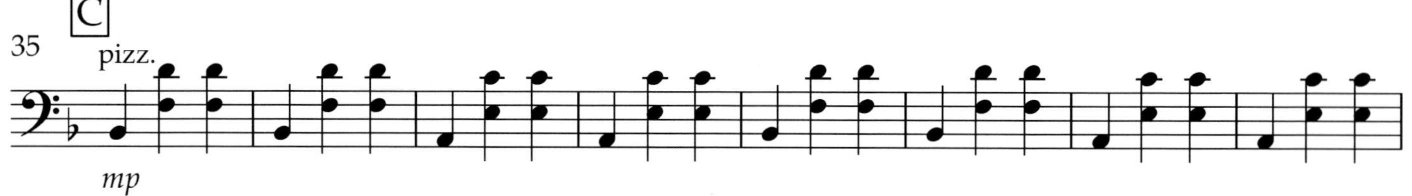

V.S.

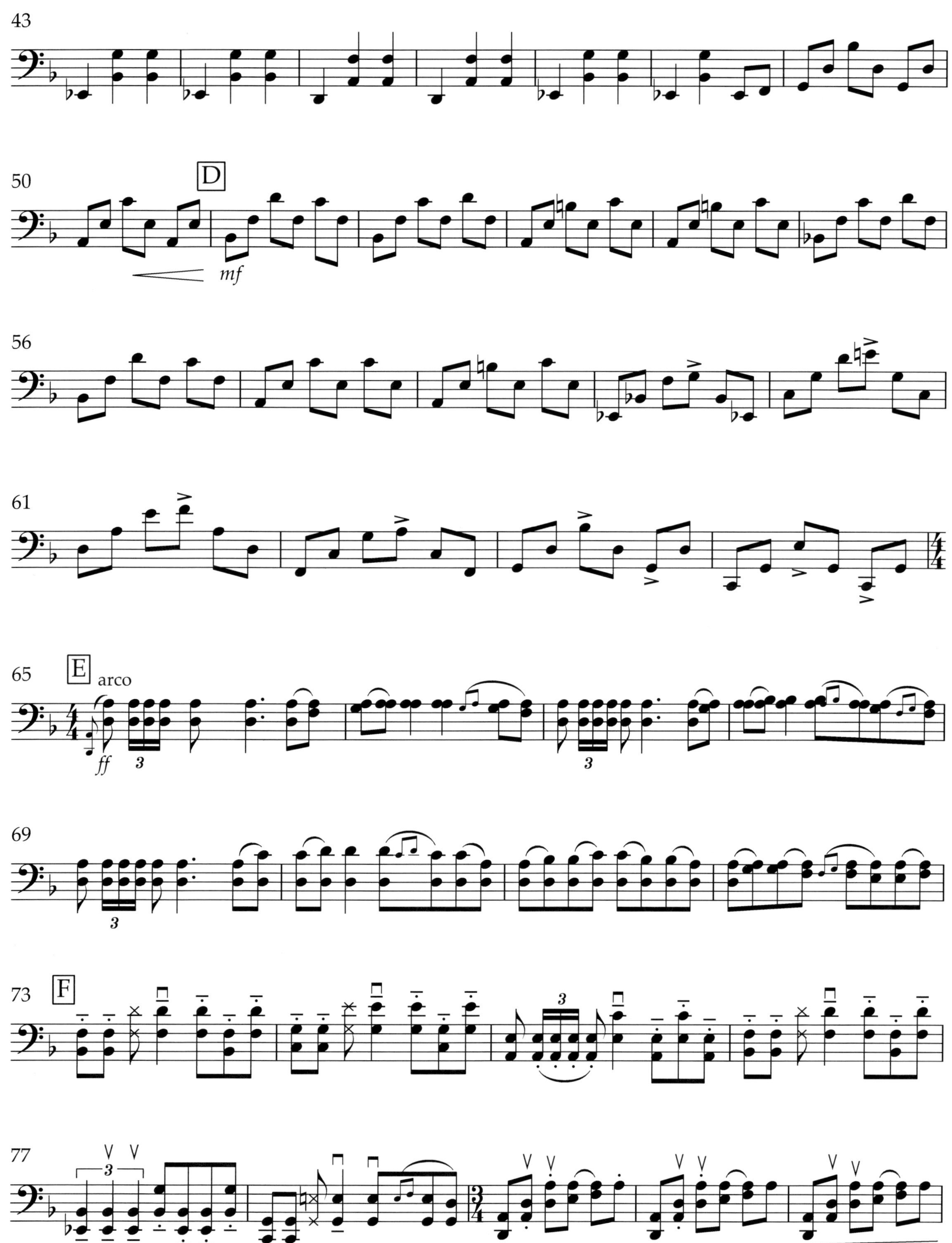
43
50
D
mf
56
61
65
E
arco
ff
3
69
73
F
77

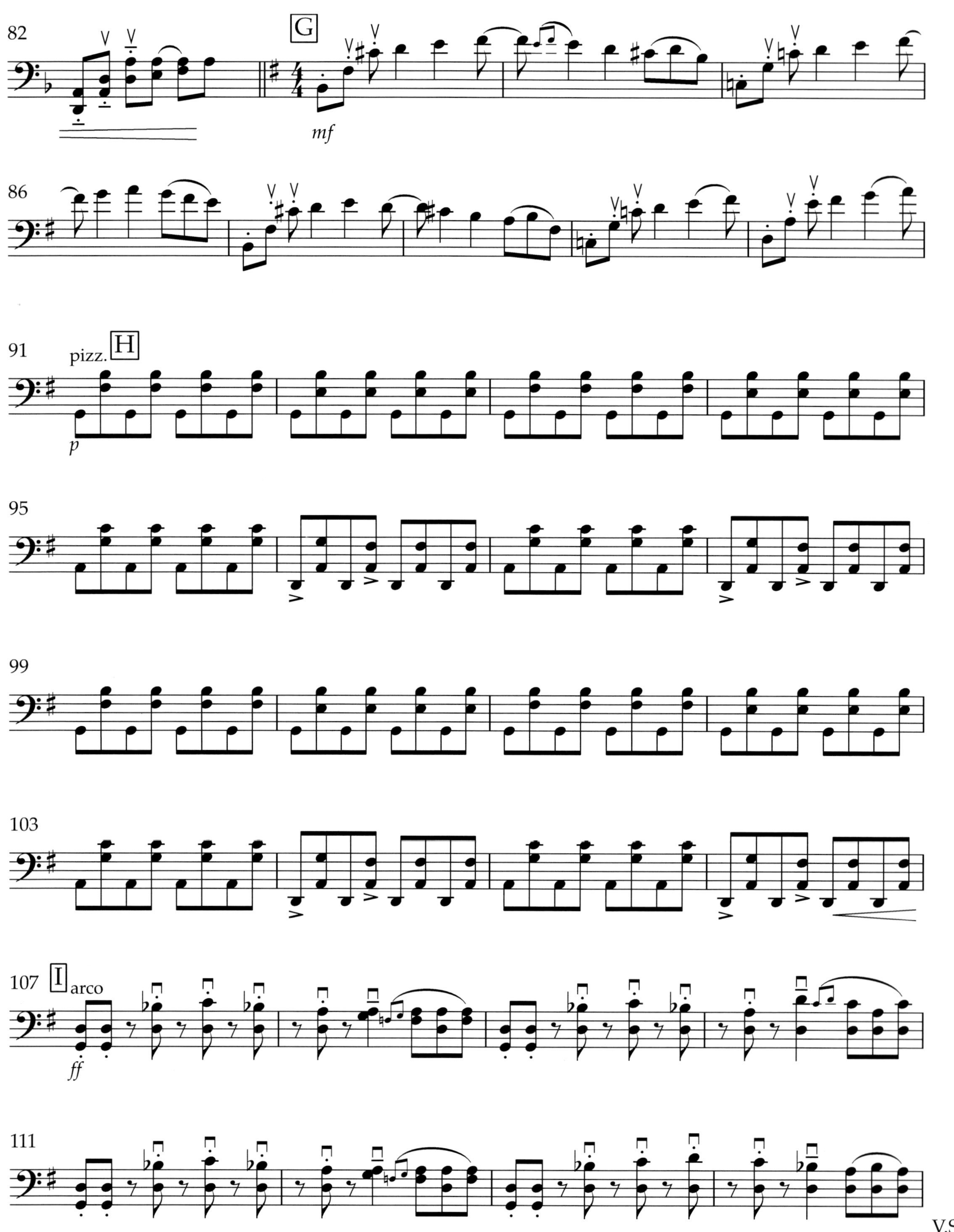

82
G
mf
86
91
pizz.
H
p
95
99
103
107
I
arco
ff
111
V.S.

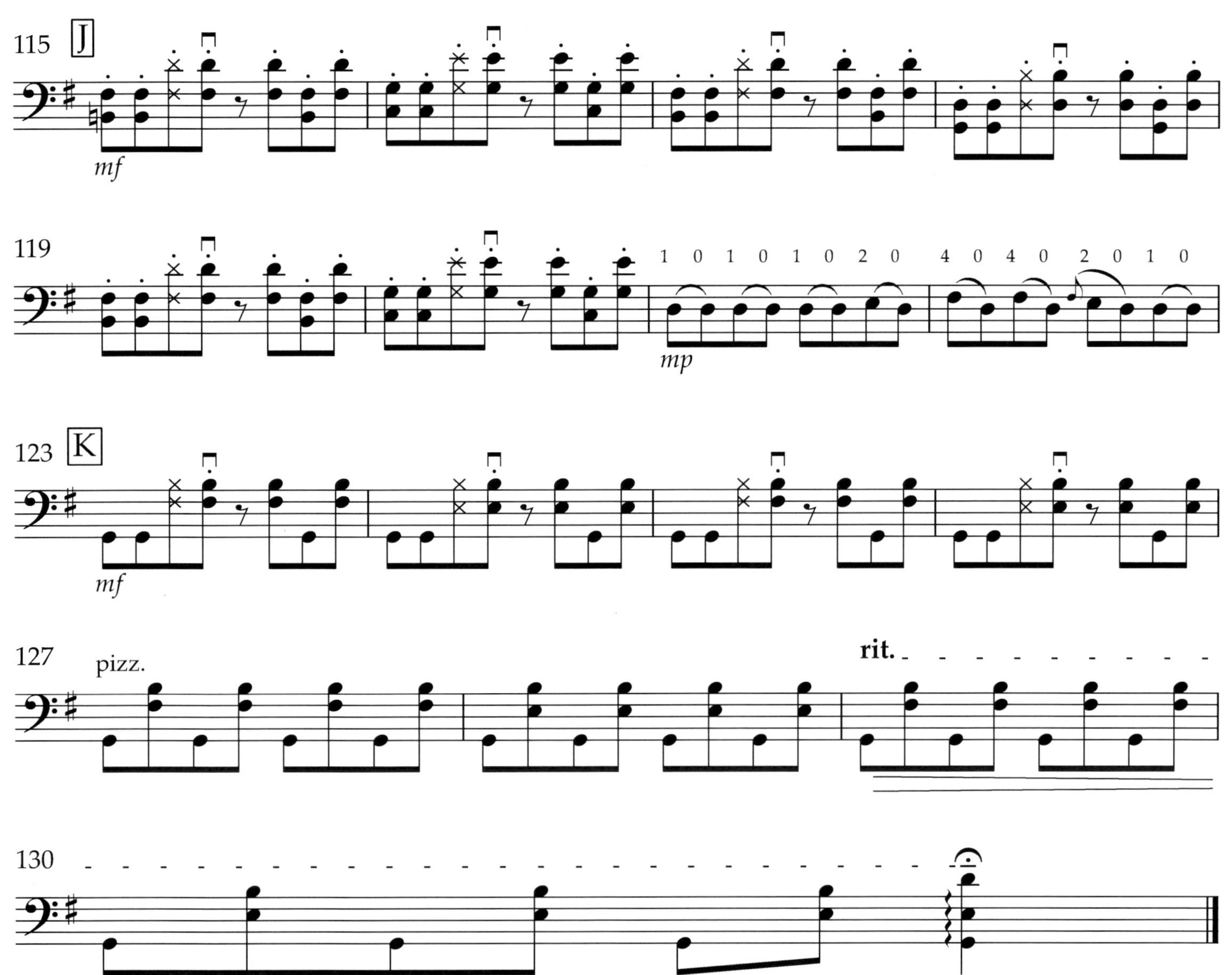
115
J
mf
119
1 0 1 0 1 0 2 0
4 0 4 0 2 0 1 0
mp
123
K
mf
127
pizz.
rit.
130

Once in Royal David's City

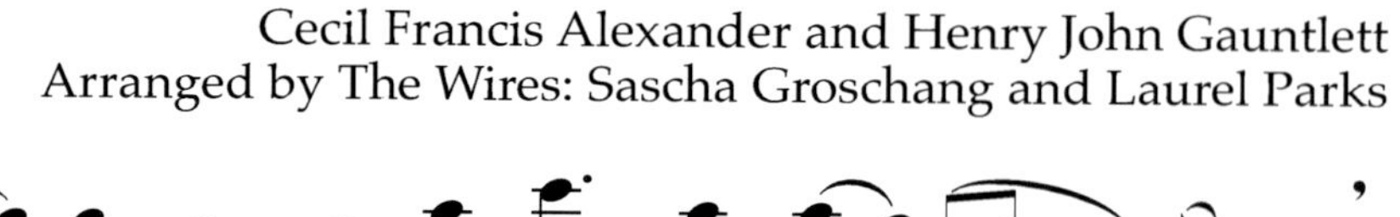

Cecil Francis Alexander and Henry John Gauntlett
Arranged by The Wires: Sascha Groschang and Laurel Parks

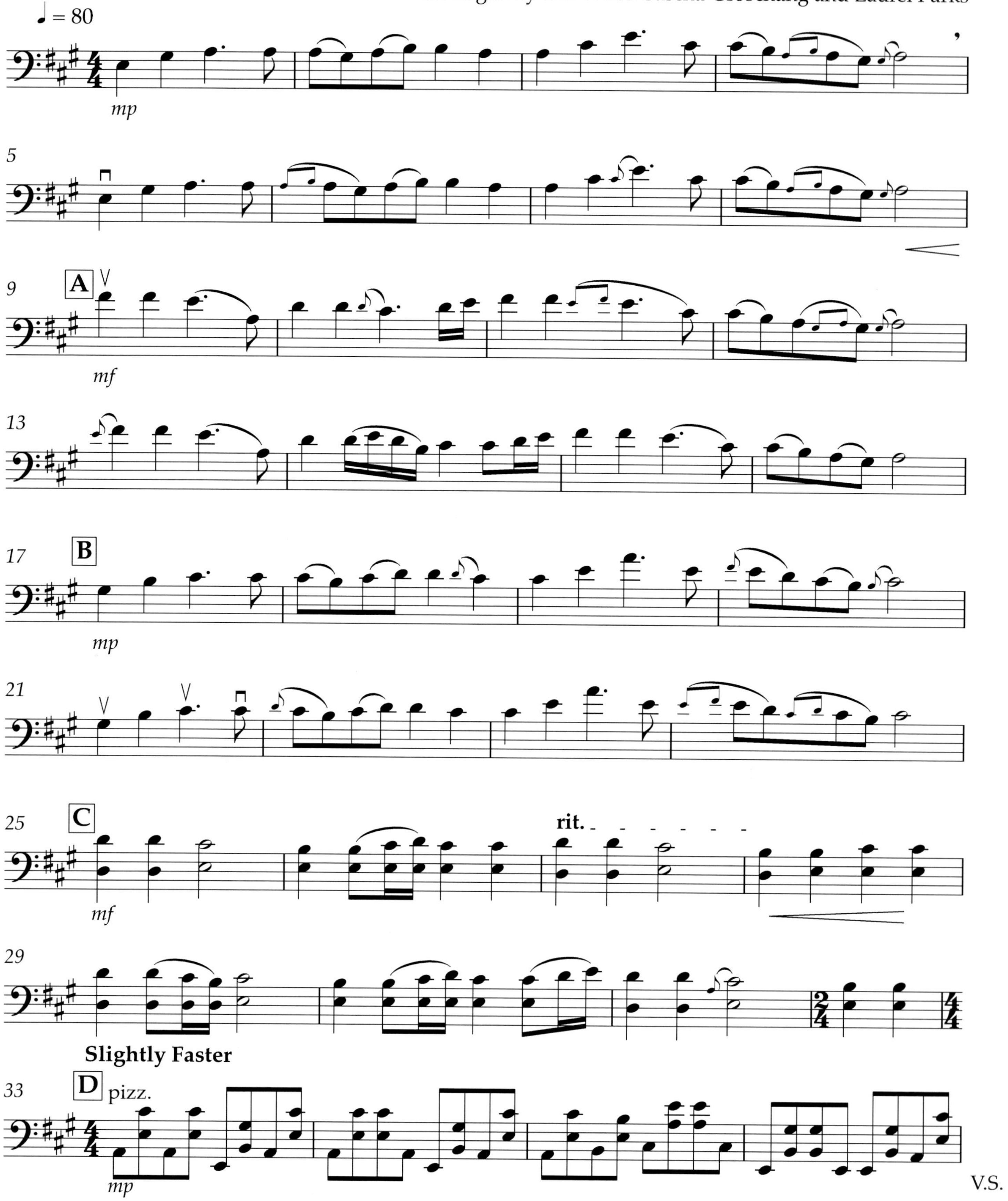

♩ = 80

mp

5

9 **A** *mf*

13

17 **B** *mp*

21

25 **C** *mf* **rit.**

29

Slightly Faster

33 **D** pizz. *mp*

V.S.

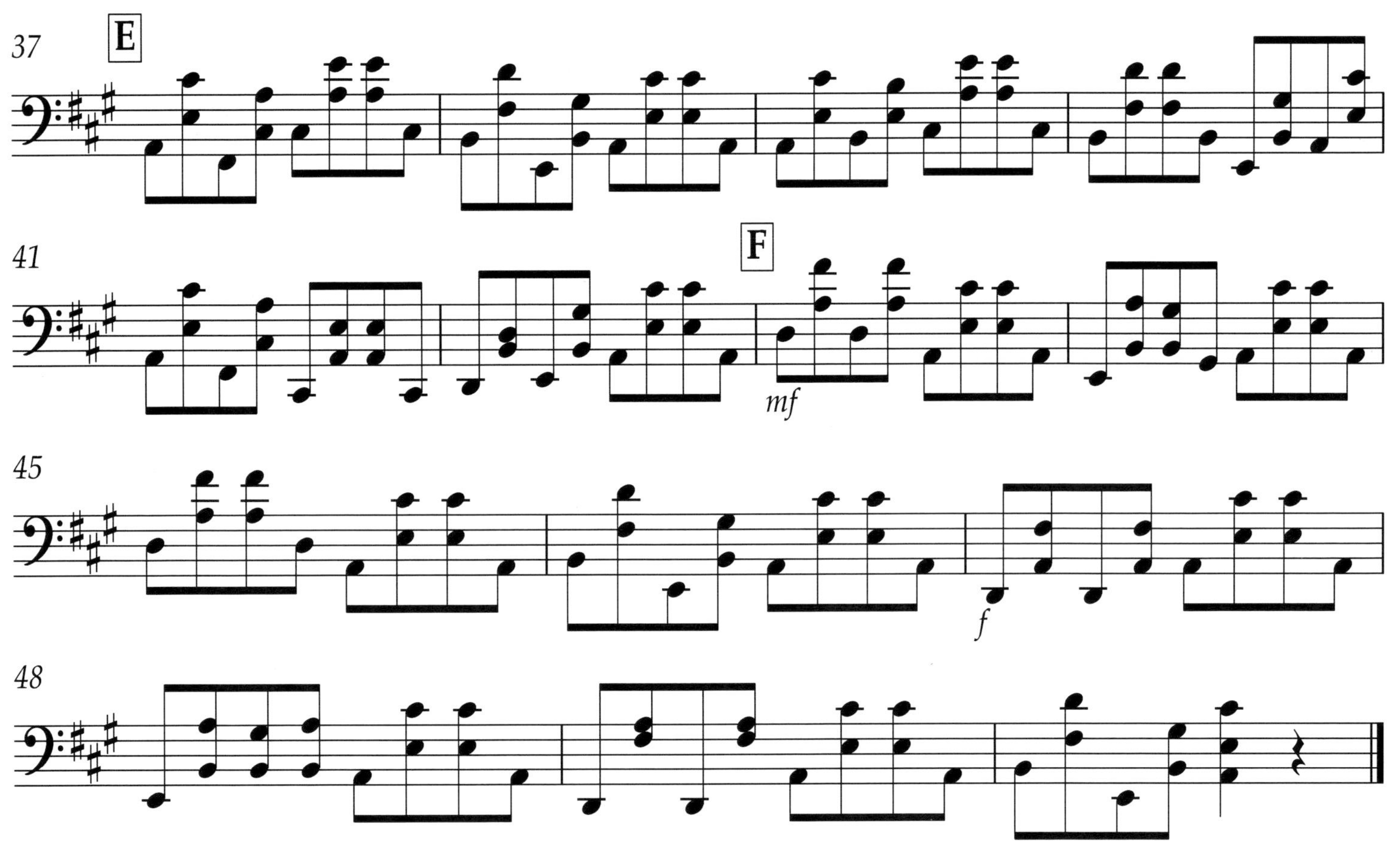
37
E
41
F
mf
45
48
f

We Wish You a Merry Christmas

Traditional English
Arranged by The Wires: Sascha Groschang and Laurel Parks

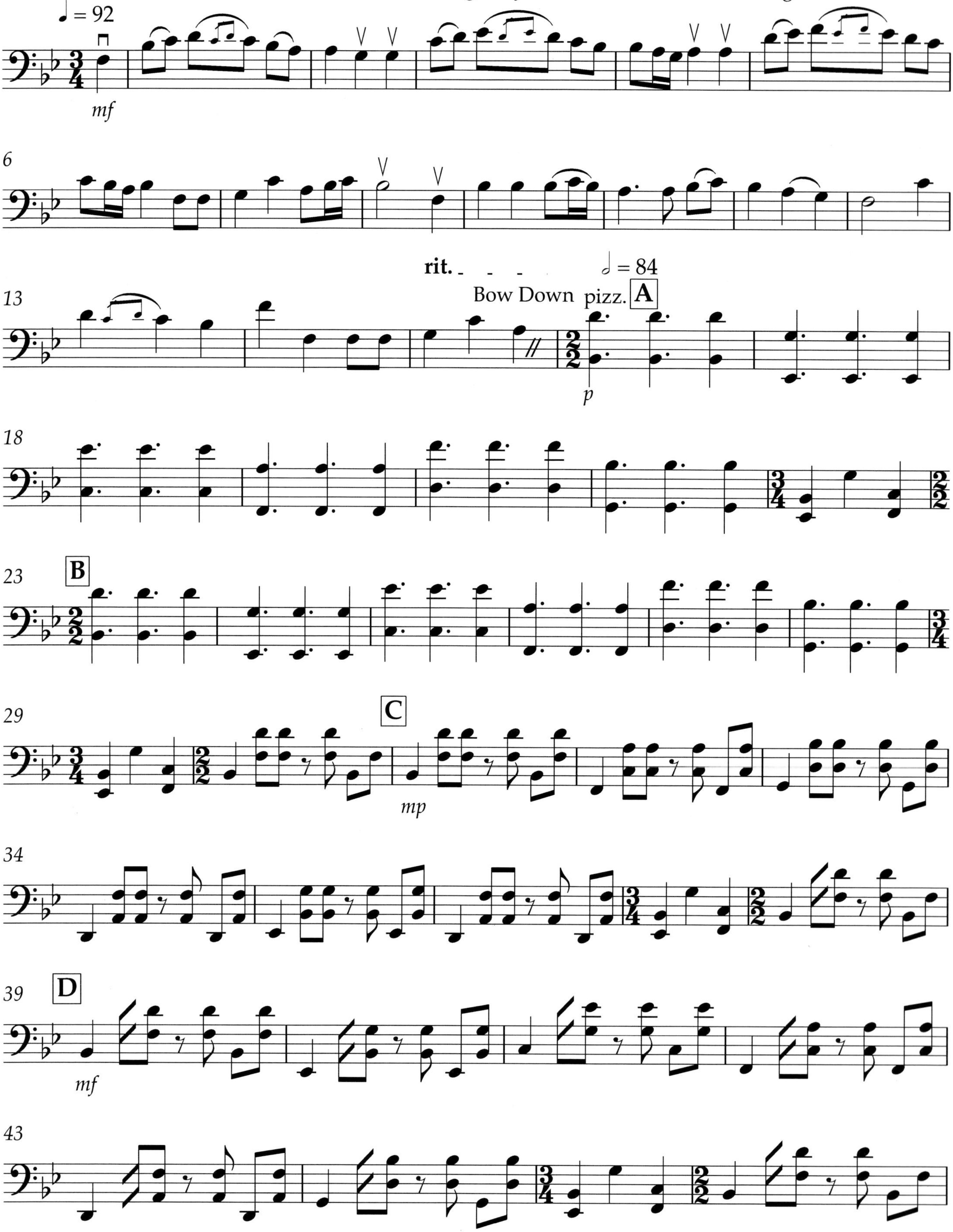

♩ = 92

mf

6

13

rit. - - - 𝅗𝅥 = 84

Bow Down pizz. **A**

p

18

23 **B**

29 **C**

mp

34

39 **D**

mf

43

V.S.

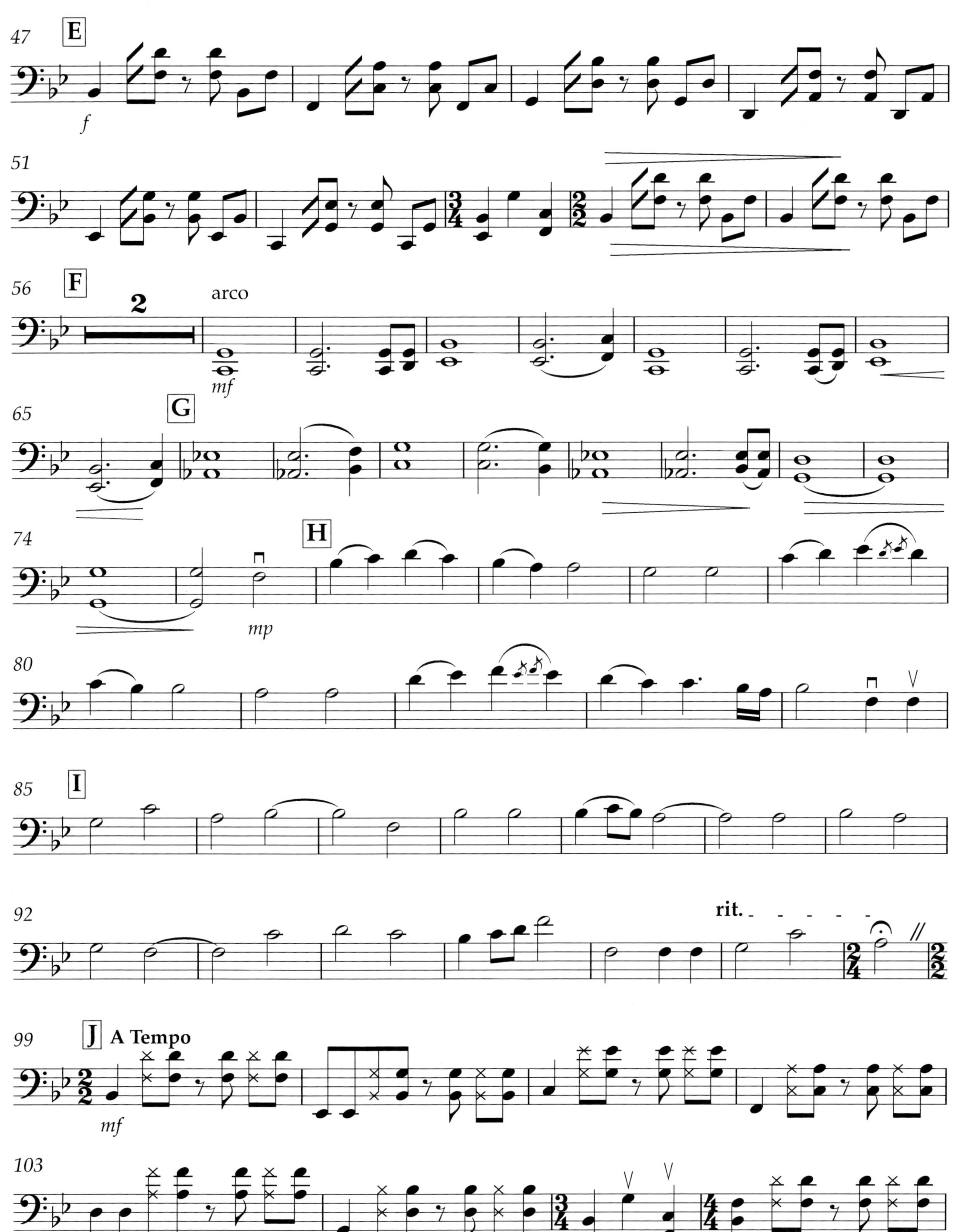

E
f
arco
mf
F
2
G
mp
H
I
rit.
J
A Tempo
mf

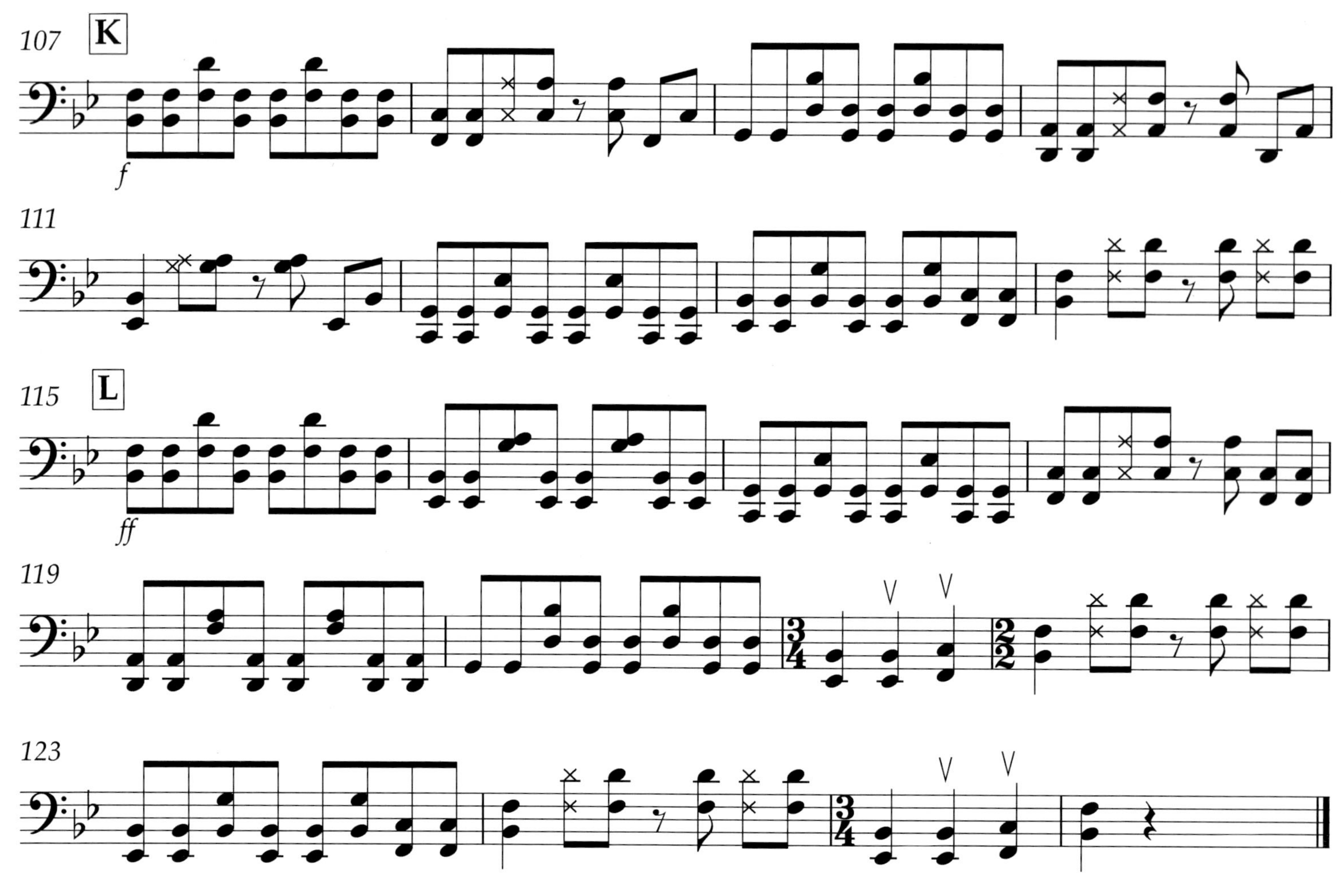
107
K
f
111
115
L
ff
119
123